COUPLE

CW00447339

No More Fighting! No More Anxiety! Effective
Communication in Relationships

(Cognitive-behavioral Therapy for Couples and
Families)

Mary Fries

Published by Oliver Leish

Mary Fries

All Rights Reserved

*Couple Therapy: No More Fighting! No More Anxiety!
Effective Communication in Relationships (Cognitive-
behavioral Therapy for Couples and Families)*

ISBN 978-1-77485-126-5

Legal & Disclaimer

Table of Contents

Introduction

This book contains proven steps and strategies on how to unleash the absolute lover within you.

...and they lived happily ever after... Have you ever wondered why fairy tale stories are so popular? Perhaps it is because they are a manifestation of what every one of us longs and hopes for; a love that can stand the test of time. A love not devoid of trials, but a love that is strong and mature enough to withstand even the biggest trial that life and the world throws at it. I do not mean to discourage your endeavors of finding love, but falling in love is just the first step to a long journey that is both happy and sad. Love is unlike anything else in this world. It has the ability to make the weirdest situations seem like a stroll down a Hawaiian beach, holding hands with your loved one, staring off into the beauty of the setting sun. Finding it, keeping it, treasuring it, and nurturing it should be something we all learn to do.

Not all of us know the formula for getting there. Nevertheless, this book will introduce you to the new world of becoming the best lover that your partner has always dreamt of having. You will be a dream come true to yourself and to your partner once you embrace the strategies discussed in this book.

Chapter 1: The Fundamentals Of Emotionally Focused Couples Therapy

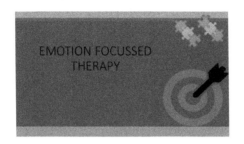

Whenever men hear the words "couple therapy," their stomachs immediately turn. They frequently feel that they'll go to treatment, they will be held responsible for the relationship's problems.

Real-Life Problem

Mike informed Angelina, "I'm not coming to couple counseling." "There's no chance. I'm going in there, and you folks are supposed to gobble me up."

The dread would be that two girls — the spouse as well as the counselor — will form a tag-team wrestling bout versus him, only this time it will be genuine. This is more like an MMA gauntlet match. There's really no going back once the cell door is locked!

Couple counseling is viewed by several men as a sheep being taken to slaughtering — and they are the sheep! Men have reason to be concerned. We've also witnessed men who have been unfairly accused. But we've seen it happen to women as well. The area of family counseling is filled with obsolete manuals from the 1970s and 1980s that portray women as the bad guys.

Emotion-focused therapy (EFT) is not like other therapies. The client in this method is the connection itself. Even though it isn't always the ideal course of action for maintaining a romantic relationship, the emotionally centered therapist thinks that couples have a legitimate reason for the actions. There are causes for your and your partner's conduct that sound right and the psychiatrist's job is to assist you and your companion figure out what they are.

1.1 Emotionally Focused Therapy: What It Is and How It Works?

In EFT, change occurs when you pay attention to your gut-level, fundamental feeling in reaction to your mate in critical relationship situations. Such deep feelings arise far too frequently beyond your normal consciousness. Whenever your partner, for instance, keeps forgetting anything crucial to you again, your pain is instantaneous. The pain is intense, and you can experience it in your body. However, the first hurt is largely supplanted with rising wrath that seeps into your veins.

Real-Life Problem

"I can't think you forgot once more!" Mason is yelled at by Mary. She gathers around her rage right afterward. Unwittingly, she presses her pain as far as her rage will allow. "How often do I need to remind you how crucial that would be to me?"

Mason is exposed to the following possibilities, which he believes are viable:

☐ **Confess and repent for his error.** This choice appears appealing, but Mason is fully aware that he may have taken this path previously, and while it was once beneficial, it no longer works. Mary is becoming increasingly irritated with him. She isn't prepared to listen to his explanations.

☐ **Decrease the significance** Mason has been extremely busy with work, despite the fact that he works for the household! He might emphasize this by claiming that remembering all is impractical. "Give a breather. Is it really that important?" Mason is well aware that this method frequently enrages Mary.

☐ **Defend yourself.** He's just human, after all! Mary is prone to forgetting things as well. In reality, she neglected to start picking up that item from the shop, which he had requested her to bring up a month ago. It was crucial to him. Perhaps she should take a step back & stop pestering him about anything and everything. The option diverts Mary's attention away from Mason and reduces the hot air on him.

However, it implies a higher vacuum in them than the previous two possibilities. If Mason chooses this path, he should expect a day or two of great uncomfortable and maybe quiet at home. That becomes tiresome.

☐ **Take it in quiet for the most part.** Mason has been hammered in his thoughts. He's made another mistake, and he's aware of it. What is he meant to do at this point?

Mason has no idea what's going on. All indicators point to Mary being even more disgusted in him, according to him. So, despite how bad he thinks on the inside, he keeps silent with the expectation that it would all go away as quickly as possible. The difficulty is that this sends the message to Mary that Mason is unconcerned.

As you've seen, neither of these solutions suit Mary and Mason's needs. In essence, neither party understands how and when to break out of such circumstances without causing harm to the other or the relationships.

Mason adds, "We are trapped in such circumstances all the time."

Mary says, "It's dreadful." "It certainly keeps occurring among us again and again."

Mason and Mary seem to have been trapped in an endless cycle of blaming, disillusionment, and pain. Everyone has a part in performing, but they can't have seemed to alter the screenplay. The partnership suffers further harm as the fights and emotional separation intensify. Mary expresses her dissatisfaction by saying, "We're drifting away." "With each quarrel, we drift more apart."

EFT is intended to break the negative patterns that lead to couples becoming unhappy, bickering, and isolating themselves from one another. Most couples fight, but when unfavorable patterns repeat themselves and get more intense, you've entered the danger zone.

EFT helps couples get beyond the surface anger and annoyance to the more susceptible feelings of hurt and fear, so reducing the destructive nature of recurrent argument cycles. Such feelings are diametrically opposed to the reactionary emotions that drive debates. They're also much more capable.

1.2 Taking into Account your Own Argumentative Cycle

Do you recognize yourself in Mason and Mary's story? Do you have a habit of arguing in the same way? Almost every couple does. Those who maintain emotional connections while working through disagreement are more likely to succeed in the long term. It doesn't mean you're not angry with each other if you're still emotionally linked.

It signifies that, despite your dissatisfaction, you are not jeopardizing your relationship. Neither of you considers the disagreement to be serious.

Activity:

Contrast your argument style with Mason and Mary's. Do you behave like Mary when you're furious with your partner? Is Mason's perspective comparable to yours if you found yourself in his shoes more frequently? Consider it independently first, and then put down your reactions:

You relate to Mason in the following methods (for instance, "You hit back whenever you hear your spouse's anger..."):

We identify with Mary in the following manner (for instance, "You appear to become upset with your spouse, and you..."):

When you've completed each of your replies, share and debate them with each other.

Real-Life Problem

During a normal dispute, neither Mason nor Mary has a clue as to how the other is truly feeling on the inside. Furthermore, during such discussions, their knowledge of their own profound emotions is hazy. The rage and fury they feel against one other is one thing they can all agree on.

Mason usually goes somewhere else in the home, outside, or on a drive after the dispute. After she and Mason dispute and emotionally separate, Mary has managed to think her own profound emotions and has experienced a genuine sensation of loneliness. "I'm first upset after we dispute, and he walks off," she adds, "but on another level, I'm terribly lonely."

Mason, obviously, is completely unaware of any of this. All he hears is an irritated Mary, who has been disappointed in him again. Mason admits, "I've screwed up again." "I failed her again."

Mary, on the other hand, has no clue what Mason suffers through when he stops fighting. He says, "It's terrible." "In my thoughts, I keep replaying the idea that I'm failing her."

Mason was eventually able to identify and feel a strong sense of Mary's failings. He was worried that she would become tired of him at some time.

Mason and Mary just cannot alleviate the tension in their interaction on their own. No quantity of communication techniques worked because we spoke one at a time and replayed what the other said back to each other. This wasn't through a lack of desire on their side, however.

It's possible that you and your spouse will end yourself in a similar scenario.

1.3   De-escalating   the   Cycle   of Confrontation

Couples learn to view one other's behaviors diversely as they start to realize and expose each other's true core feelings that lie underneath the layer of regular rage and other more reactionary emotions.

Real-Life Problem

Mason explained, "Understanding that she becomes louder if she genuinely needs me or seems as If I'm not there for her making a tremendous impact." "Which has been quite beneficial to me.

I'm starting to see past her rage, and I'm starting to see that it's hiding a more valid feeling like fear or despair. She must know that I will always be there for her.

I mean, anger is valid, but what she truly needs is something to happen beyond her fury." Mason has made a lot of improvement.

When couples continue speaking, as Mason is doing here, they begin the cycle de-escalation stage of therapy, which is known in EFT as the de-escalation phase of treatment. This essentially implies the couples sometimes dispute and fight, just not as frequently or as fiercely. Mason, for example, can face up to Mary's rage without retreating — in part since Mary's rage isn't as strong as it once was. He's also helped her see what's going on underneath her rage.

Similarly, Mary is able to "de-escalate" her rage, in part, and she no longer perceives Mason as uncaring when they argue. "I've seen what goes on inside his head when we fight," Mary explained. "He becomes agitated.

He is concerned. It's that he's not always sure how to react or what to do. It's the exact opposite of what I previously believed."

When they fought, Mary used to assume Mason didn't really care as often as she did. And with good reason: what she saw most of the time was a guy who battled with her, made an excuse, muttered a few words or even nothing, and then retreated.

"It impacted me once I witnessed how truly scared, perhaps terrified, he becomes when we make the argument," she added. Mary explained, "No one who doesn't care experiences that type of agony." "When I display too much wrath, he becomes trapped. On a certain level, he is afraid of what may happen next — having to retreat and suffer a type of suffering on his own. I seemed to have no idea what was going on in his life. "I have no idea."

Cycle de-escalation occurs as couples become aware of one another vulnerable feelings and start to explain and share them. They do not fight as much as they used to. Events among them start to shift dramatically. This stage is a natural component of the EFT healing process.

Mary expressed it perfectly, "I'm discovering that Mason isn't the adversary here." "The adversary is our tendency to hide under our wrath and annoyance rather than slowing or stopping and coping with the underlying feelings. Anxiety, isolation, and melancholy are the emotions that are provoked. That's what we really need to take care of together."

In EFT, interpersonal intimacy is developed when each partner honestly feels the other's sensitive emotions up close and personal. You "understand it" once you literally walk in your partner's underlying psychological boots. This distinguishes EFT from other forms of marital counseling.

1.4 Novel Methods to Meet Each Other

Couples generally start arguing less and less when their argument cycles reduce and settle down.

Getting to know each other better. They no longer regard the other individual as an adversary. The damaging anger, irritation, jealously, and other reactionary emotions that feed the quarrel in the first place are the adversary. Underneath the reactionary rage and irritation, the opponent hides the sensitive feelings.

When partners begin to feel closer, the path to more intimacy opens. Partners might start freely communicating their relationship needs with one another.

Whereas they may have been able to discuss requirements in the past, the situation with them was frequently stressful, and addressing "needs" was frequently greeted with reluctance.

1.5 Concern for One Another's Needs

Couples in turmoil frequently utilize "needs" to put the responsibility on one another. Mason explained, "We always had to relish hurling our desires at one other." "Like, 'I want someone who worries about me!' or 'I see you're doing this!'" she says. This was just another attempt at making the other person unhappy."

1.6 Getting to Know Each Other

Mary, too, became more candid with Mason. Rather than blaming him out of rage, she talked with him when she felt lonely and being alone. Mason was disregarded by Mary's rage. Whenever she told him she was missing him or was lonely, he felt compelled to console and convince her.

Mason stated, "Whenever she opens up towards me and tells me exactly when she's beginning to feel a touch of isolation or a slight worry, well, I'm not listening to her worries; it isn't from rage." It conveys a sense of... trepidation. It's as if she needs my assistance. It's nice to be requested."

Mason is expressing how they've been learning what everyone requires from the other through using their main or affection feeling. These really are wholesome desires that are appealing to another individual. Mason appreciates Mary's necessity for him. And Mary appreciates Mason's willingness to open out to her, allowing her to see more plainly wherever she fits within his life.

Couples who discover new methods to relate to one another and deepen their closeness realize that they will have a better relationship.

☐ Have frequent sex

☐ Have a more satisfying sex life

☐ Organize your life as a team.

☐ Count on one another to parent your children as a team.

☐ In times of distress, they can rely on one another.

- ☐ More wonderful parents
- ☐ Parents who are more effective than others
- ☐ Psychologically, they're a lot closer.
- ☐ Feel more comfortable sharing personal information with one another.
- ☐ Less arguing and fighting
- ☐ Dispute with less vigor
- ☐ Get to know each other better.

The ultimate purpose of EFT is to create a long-lasting emotional relationship among you that can weather life's earthquakes. This inner link is known as love in everyday life. EFT is about cultivating a long-lasting love between you, one that you'll have to work hard to maintain but from something, and you'll get a lot of your nourishment.

Mason responds, "We can speak about everything here." "Some of my friends can't even believe what we speak about. And that's what we've become."

1.7 Face Future Together
The final level of EFT is about a vision in which the two of you can best serve one

another by assisting each other and making choices jointly. EFT is a strong tool that, when it is used correctly and with care, may substantially aid in the strengthening of emotional ties.

Many psychological scientists place much too much emphasis on themselves and their theories. We aim to put EFT into its appropriate perspective. EFT is neither a cultural criticism nor a prescription for a better future. It's doesn't claim to be able to heal personality issues, mental illnesses, dependencies, or other mental illnesses. It isn't a replacement for faith, philosophy, or anything that comes near. It's nothing more than a notion and a strategy for bringing individuals closer emotionally.

1.8 Taking on Difficult Problems as a Team

Past difficulty areas become easier to manage whenever partners are at peace with one other rather than at odds. This is due to the fact that partners collaborate rather than compete.

"I'll stay for a drink or a snack a lot now," Mason adds, "and I'll end up making sure to buy anything for her as well." A box of gum and a chocolate bar, both of which I understand she enjoys but seldom purchases for herself. I'd like to do stuff like this anyway."

It is not thoughts for solving issues that are important in EFT. It's about bringing the world of you as well and putting you on the very same path on a stronger connection base, so you can work together to tackle old difficulties.

Chapter 2: How Emotions Affect Your Partner

Anger is a normal human emotion but a powerful one for that matter. It is essential to show frustration, hurt, disappointment, and annoyance with other people, including romantic partners. It is healthy for you to express anger when aggrieved by your partner, but you should do it in a controlled way.

When you express anger in unhealthy ways, you not only hurt your partner, but you also prevent yourself from conveying what exactly your problem with the situation you are in is. When you express anger in unhealthy ways, you also damage your relationship and make it impossible to salvage the once healthy, loving relationship you had with your partner.

Unmanaged anger also interferes with the quality of life that you lead as it affects your physical and mental health. To avoid all this, people can learn to control their anger. It is possible to manage anger in healthier ways. Here are a few ways to do so.

Once you're Calm, Express Your Anger

When your partner aggrieves you, it is crucial for you to let your anger subside before confronting him or her. This ensures that you do not say something that you cannot take back in the heat of an argument. If you cannot get away, try taking some deep breaths before you speak to the person.

Once you have your emotions under control, try to pinpoint exactly why you are upset or what exactly has set off the feelings that you are feeling. There are times when people get irritable because of other things that are happening in their lives.

You can begin by first telling the other person how difficult the situation is for you. By doing this, you disarm them and force them to show you empathy, which means that they also get distracted and forget about their anger.

Once both of you are calm, you can continue to explain the reason why you are upset and convey precisely what you are mad about. In the process, you should also talk about the emotions that you are feeling and how the other person's actions affect you. You should also focus on the current problem and not what mistakes your partner did in the past. If you, at any point, sense that your anger is beginning to rise, take a break. This gives you time to cool down and gather back your thoughts. You can also try counting one to ten as you practice some heavy breathing.

As you speak, be assertive but not hostile. Assertive communication involves stating only that which is factual without pointing accusations at the other person. As you point out an issue or issues, do not talk in a confrontational way, this can agitate the other party and cause them to react in anger. When you speak while calm, the other person is also able to listen and understand what you are saying.

Once you finish giving all your concerns, you should also provide the other party the same opportunity to state their case and the reason behind their actions. Try to see things from their perspective before you react in any way. Both of you should listen to one another keenly and repeat what you think the person means to gain a better understanding of each other.

Take A Timeout

Anger clouds people's judgment, so it is always a good idea to take time out of a confrontational situation to calm down. Timeout also gives the other person the same space to thinks about the issue at hand. Depending on the problem, the timeout can be as brief as a few minutes or can last even a few days. In a short timeout, people can practice some quick relaxing techniques. Some quiet time away, even in front of your partner, can give both of you time to cool down.

Counting to 100 can also help to take your mind off the situation and reset. After the timeout, you can begin to gather your thoughts calmly again. Anytime you sense like you are about to explode, you can get away and take a short walk outside or around the block to clear your head.

Exercise is also an excellent way to blow off steam. You can choose to go for a run or have an intense work out session at the gym. A high-energy consuming activity like boxing or martial arts, will distract and exhaust you to the point that you forget about your problem for a while.

Breathing exercises can also be beneficial, especially if coupled with an activity like yoga. However, you should look for something that you enjoy doing which you know can relax you.

You can also talk to a third party to vent out your anger and the frustrations you are undergoing in your relationship. This person can simply lend a listening ear, but they can also give a better perspective of the situation and reaffirm or try to change your perception of the case. The person can also help you to identify the exact cause of your feelings clearly.

Any activity that works to distract or calm you down like a shower, writing, listening to music is also worth a try.

Identify Possible Solutions

As you try to work out your issues with your partner, look for solutions to your problem instead of dwelling on the problem. If you find yourself always getting irritated with your partner because of a particular habit or situation, remove yourself from the trigger. Getting upset all the time does not help in dealing with life's frustrations.

You can decide to change your reaction towards other people's actions and in this case, your partner. Challenge your thinking and get down to the root cause of your anger. Identify the thought patterns that lead you to violence and change them. Make a decision to let go of situations that you cannot control as well as angry thoughts. You can also try to develop resilience in conditions that have the potential of making you angry.

Taking care of both your psychological and physical health on a daily basis also ensures that you are able to deal with people in the right way. People who are always stressed find themselves getting angry too often and too quickly. Daily exercises, even for a few minutes in a day, can help relax your body and burn out any stress that you might be experiencing. Meditation and deep breathing exercises also help in relaxing your body. Taking breaks to go for a holiday or enjoy a day out can help relax your mind.

Quality sleep also gives your body time to relax and rejuvenate in order to be able to handle any stressors or challenges that come your way. Experts advocate for at least 8 hours of sleep on a daily basis. Substance use and alcohol consumption also impair a person's ability to make sound decisions and reason, therefore avoid them if you can. You should also keep the consumption of high-energy drinks and caffeine at minimum levels to avoid being irritable.

Self-help books and self-help programs can also teach you anger management skills as well as healthier ways of expressing anger.

If you still find yourself incapable to control your anger with any of the above techniques and you keeping hurting your significant other, you can enroll for anger management classes to help you cope with your anger issues. Such levels advise and teach you healthier ways of managing your anger. Depending on how out of control your passion is, you can sign up for a one-off class, a weekend program, or a one-month program. Until you are able to manage your anger, you should seek all the possible help you can get.

Therapy is also an option. Psychologists can help people deal with other underlying issues that may contribute to them always feeling angry.

Do Not Hold a Grudge

Once you and your partner address a particular issue, you should close that chapter and move on. If you cannot agree with your partner, you can always agree to disagree and move on with life. You can also decide to ignore your partner's shortcomings and find a way of living with them. Another way to distract yourself is to focus on the good qualities your partner has. This takes your mind off things that irritate you.

Whatever way you choose to take, you should not keep dwelling on past issues, and neither should you keep bringing up past mistakes in future conversations or arguments with your partner. Holding grudges and reminding each other of one another's errors or listing each other wrongdoings will only escalate anger.

You should also practice forgiveness. Forgiveness has the power to heal you as well as the other party. When you forgive a person, they are likely to become conscious of their mistakes, and this can lead them to make a point of never repeating them again. Forgiveness also makes both parties let go of any negative feeling that they may have, which gives room for the healing process to begin.

Agreeing on healthy ways to resolve issues in your relationship also prevents couples from going at each other in the future. Couples should even know the difference between letting things go and suppressing their anger. Repressing anger is unhealthy in relationships. If you still feel resentment towards your partner, then chances are you are controlling some issues with your partner, and you need to be open about them to avoid exploding at your partner in the future.

Holding on to anger also affects the quality of life that you live and interferes with your physical, mental health, and overall well-being. Constant anger floods your body with stress hormones that increase heart rate and blood pressure. With time, recurrent passion can lead to heart disease, stroke, and psychological disorders.

Use Humor to Release Tension

You can use humor to change the mood in an otherwise tense room, but you should use it creatively, or it can end up doing more harm than good. You should never laugh at the other person's mistakes, their weakness, or their lack of sound judgment. Do not insult their intelligence or way of thinking. The other party may become upset and make a regrettable statement, which will only fuel the anger that both of you are currently dealing with.

You should avoid sarcasm or bad jokes that are insulting. Instead, try to direct most of the fun at yourself or at the situation. Self-deprecating humor, when dealing with anger, is used to remind the other people that everyone has flaws and can make mistakes, so they should not feel too bad about their wrongdoings.

When you use humor well, it can disarm the other party and bring his or her defenses down. Humor also prevents the two parties from hurting each other's feelings. It also reduces any tension between the two people, which creates a situation where both parties can begin to discuss the issue at hand and come to an agreement.

Silent humor can also help you cope with your anger. For example, you can draw a mental picture of your partner as a tiny mischievous cartoon devil with horns. You can choose to share the image with your partner or not, but in either case, the funny cartoon image can help distract you from your anger.

Chapter 3: Understanding Couple Relationship And Its Purpose

The definition of "relationships" is broad, and differs from individual to individual. What you think about the relationship is special to you, but the majority of the people think of a connecting state, especially an emotional connection.

Personal relationships relate to close interpersonal connections, created by emotional bonds and interactions. These bonds often develop from and are reinforced by some mutual experiences.

Relationships are not constant; they evolve continuously, and we need skills, information, motivation, practice and social support to fully enjoy and benefit from them. There are three sorts of personal relationships i.e.

· Family
· Friends
· Partnership (Couples)

Couples or partnerships, especially marriage, are intimate relationships founded upon friendship, confidence, affection, and romantic love between two individuals. Such kind of relationship usually is an encounter with just one person at a time.

1.1 What is Couple Relationship?

If humans had to be alone and happy with the inherent characteristic, maybe the population would be much less, and each of us would occupy our own personal island. Fortunately, however, and sadly, we are highly developed individuals for whom a basic imperative is to love and be loved. It is, therefore, a choice that we want to be in a partnership to ensure to live our life happily ever after.

Relationships are an important part of healthy living, but such a thing as a perfect relationship does not exist. From friends to romances, relationships have the potential to enrich our lives and contribute to our enjoyment of life. Those same relationships, however, can cause discomfort, and sometimes even harm.

Healthy Vs Unhealthy Relationship

Healthy relationships awn both partners to feel supported and connected and also feel
independent. Communication and bounda ries are the two primary units of a healthy relationship among the persons. The two people in the relationship actually decide what's fit for them, and what's not. If something doesn't feel right, your partner will have the ability to access your concerns.

What Builds A Healthy And Successful Relationship?

A healthy and successful relationship is when two people develop a connection based on:

· Mutual respect
· Trust
· Honesty
· Support
· Fairness/equality
· Separate identities
· Good communication
· A sense of playfulness/fondness

These are all things that take work. It is most likely that any relationship blends

both healthy and unhealthy features. Relationships must be maintained, and stable relationships must be established. This refers to all ties, working relationships, friendships, and relationships with the family and romance.
What Are The Signs Of A Healthy Relationship?

A stable relationship will bring your life more joy than stress. Each relationship often has tension, but you want to avoid excessive stress and anxiety on either partner.

Below are some of the features of a healthy relationship.

· Take better care of yourself and be self-confident regardless of your relationship
· Maintain and respect the individuality of each other
· Maintain friends and family relationships
· Have different and separate activities
· You can express yourself without fear of the consequences
· Should feel safe and relaxed
· Allow other relationships and encourage them

· Take an interest in the activities of each other
· Don't worry about relationship violence
· Confide and be frank with one another
· Have privacy option
· Honor personal boundaries
· Be frank about sexual activity during sexual relations
· Take influence. Relationships are important for your partner, it can be terribly challenging for some men to influence you
· Equal dispute resolution
· Even stable partnerships are part of the war, and the difference is the way the dispute is treated. Combating equally is a valuable ability that helps you establish healthy relationships.

What Are The Common Signs Of An Unhealthy Relationship?

Often all relationships have any of the following characteristics. Unhealthy relationships, however, are more frequent and cause pressure and stress that are difficult to avoid. This conflict is unhealthy for both partners and can lead to troubles in other aspects of life.

· Before one person, neglect yourself or your partner

· Feel pressure to improve who you are for someone else

· Feel worried when the other person disagrees

· Feel the pressure to stop your usual activities

· Press the other person to agree or change to fit you better

· Note that one of you must justify your actions (for example, where you go, who you see)

· Notice a partner is obliged to have sex or is forced to have sex

· You or your partner refuse safer sexual practices

· Arguments for notifications are not fairly settled

· Screaming experience or physical violence during an argument

· Attempt to manipulate or dominate one another

· Note that your partner is trying to control your clothes and criticizes your behavior
· Do not spend time with each other
· Do not have familiar friends or show respect for the friends and family of each other
· Note unequal resource control (e.g. food, money, home, car, etc.)
· Lack of equity and equality

If any of your relationships have the characteristics as mentioned above, it doesn't actually mean the end of that relationship. You will start work on changing the negative dimension of your relationships to your advantage by understanding how those characteristics impact you.

1.2 Why Relationship Matters?

From the time we are infants, we are wired to link to others. In the earliest experience of the infant, the caregiver consistently meets the child's food, treatment, comfort, security, stimulation and social interaction needs. These relationships are not inherently good or bad but are theoretical to develop deeply rooted patterns of relationships with others. Often we will withdraw from many other people when we face challenges. However, strengthening our relationships with people will change our feelings and thoughts for the better rather than retiring.

Whether they are friends, family members or partners, mentors or colleagues, your relationships can also be great for your mental wellbeing.

Love is one of human beings' most substantial feelings. There is a lot of passion, but often people want to express themselves in a romantic partnership with a happy partner.

For several, romantic relationships represent one of the most significant aspects of life, a source of profound fulfillment. A need for human relationships seems innate, but the capacity to build healthy and loving relationships is managed to learn.

Failed relationships occur for many reasons, and a relationship failure is often a cause of great mental anguish. Most people must actively learn to develop the skills required to survive and succeed in relationships.

You can also get closer to others in your life by closely connecting with only one person. Let's see how developing relationships will help and what you can do to maintain that relationship.

Remember How Other People Can Help

When you suffer from a hard time, then, good healthy and successful relationships can:

Offer Your Support

If you have been suffering, it's nice to talk about what you feel with family and friends. People care and are there to help you, listen and assist you in action. But you don't have to say all to any of it. For starters, if you face a few mental health problems, it's all right to tell a few friends, not others.

Take Your Mind off Things

Sometimes we can get stuck inside our heads or fall into unhelpful habits. Doing things with your fellows is a great way to take care and help you feel very much like yourself.

Help You Feel Less Solitary

As we speak to people about what we're doing, it's always interesting how often they can relate to us. Everybody is special, but realizing that other persons have had similar experiences may be genuinely comforting.

1.3 Types of Couple Relationship

Eventually, you expect to find someone or somebody whose favorite type of relation is like yours. First of all, it helps to learn how to be in a relationship in all different ways.

Following are the seven most rising forms of relationships you want to learn while you are in the world of relationship:

Monogamous Relationships

Monogamous relationships seem to be the first which people know because they are the most common and most straightforward for children to recognize who often see their parents showing them. Those who are in monogamous relationships have only one sexual/romantic partner. Most people who engage in "traditional" connections and marriages do so because they always want to be monogamous, though they don't always stay that way.

Polyandrous Relationships

This is why some people instead choose to have polyandrous relationships. If someone is multifaceted, it indicates they have more than one romantic relationship at a time. Sometimes polyandrous couples have a main partner, a secondary partner, etc., recognizing that such "rankings," like their needs, will alter. Others treat every relationship they engage in simultaneously as perfectly equal. Honest and effective communication between all parties is the key to any successful relationship, but particularly polyandrous.

Open Relationships

Open relationships are, in several respects, a combination between monogamous and polyandrous relations. While an open relationship enables both partners to experience physical intimacy with everyone they choose, but they maintain emotional intimacy with each other. So every individual can have as many sex partners as they would like, but only one romantic partner.

Long-Distance Relationships

A long-distance relationship is very self-explanatory, as it only occurs when partners have a long distance from each other. Because the couple's physical distance causes a lack of intimacy, some people choose to open up their relationship while living far apart. Although the "long-distance" part of this type of relationship is often short term, some couples may choose to live happily forever separate.

Casual Sex Relationships

In casual sex, both partners agree to sex on a daily basis, and that's what it is. Those in casual relationships can be intimate with each other physically and/or emotionally if both persons are comfortable. Casual sex may also be "only," that is to say, no one sleeps with anyone else, equivalent to monogamous relations without emotional connections.

43

Friends with Benefits Relationships

A "friends with benefits" relationship looks like a casual, with one important difference, i.e. a strong, platonic friendship. "Friends with benefits" relationships often start with a mutual sexual attraction between two friends. The partners behave strictly platonically outside the sexual relationship. In general, a relationship between 'friends with benefits' ends when one or both partners start dating someone else.

Asexual Relationships

Some people are asexual, which means that they do not feel any sexual desire or attraction, but still want to engage in a romantic relationship. Although asexual people often prefer to make a strictly asexual relationship between themselves to date, this is not always the case. If an asexual person and a sexual person enter into a relationship, the visibility and education network of Asexuality can take a few different forms. The pair can choose to be entirely sexless, or the asexual partner can compromise in such situations by engaging in sex occasionally, or couples may experiment "pseudo-sexual behavior" such as cuddling to find a solution for both.

Chapter 4: Concept Of Couples Therapy

The following ideas can help you identify the areas we work in and encourage discussion between you and your partner between meetings. If you regularly review this list, you will find that your thoughts and connections will change over time. So please check this list often, it will help you focus during our work.

Attitude is the key. When it is time to improving your relationship, your approach to change is more important than the action you take. What next and how to do it can regularly be no problem at all recognised. To the right

The challenge is, why not. Thinking about a problem differently is often more effective than just trying to figure out what to do.

Your partner has a somewhat limited ability to respond to you. You have a somewhat limited ability to respond to a partner. Accepting it is a big step towards maturity. There is a definite possibility that you have misconceptions about your partner's motivations. And that he/she has misconceptions about yours. The issue is that more often than not, we don't want to believe that these assumptions are wrong.

Focus on changing yourself instead of your partner

Couple therapy works best if you have more goals for yourself than for a partner. I am at my best to help you achieve the goals you have set for yourself. Problems arise when reality abruptly deviates from our expectations, hopes, desires and concerns. Try human nature

and change partners instead of adapting to our expectations. This part of human instinct is the thing that keeps specialists in the business. The hardest part of couple therapy is accepting that you will need to improve your response to the problem (how you think about it, how you feel, or then again what to do about it). Not very many individuals need to concentrate on improving their reaction. It is more common to build a substantial file to explain why another should improve. You cannot change partners. Your partner cannot change you. They can influence each other, but they don't

They can change. Becoming a more effective partner is the most effective way to improve your relationship. It is easy to be considerate and to love your partner when the view is magnificent, the sun is shining, and the breeze is soft. But when the bones get cold,

you are hungry and tired, and your partner is complaining and complaining about putting them in this mess, he will test you. His leadership and character have been verified. You can join the pointer or become what you want. Nothing is impossible for a person who does not need it. Fear lets you know that you are not ready. If you see the fear in this mode, it becomes a signal to prepare yourself as well as possible. You can learn a lot about yourself by understanding what is bothering you and how you manage it. The more you think your partner should be different, the less you will take to change the patterns between you.

Zen aspects of couple therapy (some contradictions)

All primary goals have inherent inconsistencies, for example, in speaking or maintaining peace. Any significant growth comes from disagreement, dissatisfaction with the current situation or an effort to improve things. Paradoxically, the acceptance of this conflict generates growth and

Learning to resolve inevitable differences is the key to more harmonious relationships. This is not what you say. This is what they hear. The solutions, as they stand, open the door to new problems.

Difficult questions

Asking the right questions, you and your partner will help you identify the underlying causes. Do you believe that your partner is entitled to his opinion? Under coercion, do you have the fearlessness and perseverance to seek the reality of your partner?

What's more, the boldness to communicate your existence when a lot is on the line? For what reason is it essential for your partner to know what he thinks, feels and cares about? (Since they genuinely can't acknowledge what they don't comprehend). How much will your partner have to pay to improve your response? How interested are you in the value they should pay? (Everything has a cost, and we generally pay it). Could you genuinely anticipate that your accomplice should treat you superior to he/she? Can you honestly expect that your accomplice should manage you better than yourself? If you want your partner to change, are you considering what you can do to make it easier? When the problem arises, it is natural to think "What should I do?" Much more productive is the question: "How are you trying to be in this situation?"

The importance of communication.

The three most significant characteristics for successful correspondence are regard, receptiveness and determination. Excellent communication is substantially more troublesome than the vast majority think.

Negotiating effectively is even more difficult. The couple's vision comes from the process of reflection and questioning. Both require talking from the bottom of your heart about what matters.

We are all responsible for our expression, no matter how others treat us.

Communication is the number one problem in counselling couples. Effective communication means that you need to pay attention to:

Handle indecent emotions, such as overly intense anger.

How do you communicate: complaints, blame, vague, etc.

What you expect from your partner during the discussion

What the problem symbolises for you

The result you expect from the discussion

The main concerns of your partner

How you can help your partner react more

Beliefs and attitudes towards the problem.

No wonder excellent communication is so difficult.

You cannot create a flourishing relationship by correcting what is wrong. But this is the start grace under pressure does not reach its full growth with the best intentions: practice, practice and more practice. Practice the right things, and you will arrive.

Love is pulverised when the rules of self-initiation

If you don't know how you feel in critical areas of your relationship, it's like playing high-stakes poker when you only see half of your cards. You will make a lot of stupid games

There is an option to choose the partners we need, but we don't necessarily have to get to the bottom of the problem often means that you first accept the complexity of trust that is the foundation of a flourishing relationship. You build confidence by doing what you say you will do

It is impossible to be in a highly interdependent relationship without being judged or judged. If you try always to feel secure in your relationship and it does happen, you will pay the price for it by being bored. If none of you has ever the rocks will be shipped, and you will end up with an energetic relationship knowledge is not power. The only experience that applies is power.

The majority of the useless things we do seeing someone fall into a few categories:

Blame or try to dominate

Release / delete

Boring deal

to complain

Denial or confusion

These are normal emotional reactions to feelings of threat or high stress. Improving your relationship also means better managing these reactions. Everything you do works for one part of you, even if other parts don't like it. Three motivations fuel everything you do in a persistent effort:

Avoid pain or discomfort.

The benefits involved

Be a better person The same goes for your partner

If you are asking your partner to change something, it is sometimes a good idea to ask if the change is consistent with how you are trying to be in this situation. Businesses and marriages fail for the same three reasons. Failed in:

Learn from the past

Adapt to changing conditions.

Anticipate likely future problems and take action.

Effective change requires vision and action. Action without insight is reckless. Perception without action is passivity. In the case that you need to make a successful win arrangement, you can't keep the position that your partner has lost in the past.

Examine Your Commitment Before Seeking Couples Therapy

Often when a couple is in a conflict or divorce, couple therapy may seem like a good idea. After all, what can hurt an expert to resolve his differences and put him on the path to happiness? It is not that simple. While therapy can do great things between you and your spouse, it can only happen if you are both ready and open to the obligations you will take on.

Without the right commitment, therapy sessions are doomed to failure from the start, and it will cost you a bundle to accomplish nothing. Before seeking professional help in the hope of a positive outcome, you should both consider three key questions.

Challenge yourself if you invest time and money. No one says that therapy is natural, and you will have to talk about some harrowing subjects to get to the bottom of your problems. The sessions will be invited each time and will not be excused. The only answer is to find everything, and you can only decide if you have the stamina and the strength to see everything. Occupational therapy is expensive. Can you afford it in the long run? This will not create a strong and healthy marriage in just one or two sessions so that it will be a constant expense for the foreseeable future.

Are you a reasonable person ready to commit? If you have already concluded that you are always right and that your spouse is still wrong, you do not leave much room for change. In all marriages, both partners have weaknesses that they must work on. Can you accept that from you? The will to take the deficiencies with a positive and voluntary attitude is crucial for success. No one wants to live with someone who is always right and admit defeat in every fight. If you've never wanted to commit and seek common ground, couple therapy is probably not for you.

Are you open to new ideas and suggestions? Be honest now. If you find that you are adamant and unable to adapt to the change, therapy will not work for you. Your therapist will meet the two of you and suggest new concepts that you can work with to change the status quo. Don't just go to sessions thinking that an expert can magically change your marriage in a working relationship. It will take work, and you and your spouse will have to do it. A receptive outlook and an ability to team up and change are the tools you will need to succeed.

Marriage counselling and therapy for couples

As the world becomes very glamorous, more relationships and marriages are on the brink. Husbands and wives disagree on many issues and often resort to divorce without the effort of seeking solid marriage counselling from a trusted relationship expert. Some even avoid effective couple therapy or withdrawal, while others are just not too embarrassed to seek marriage counselling. When will people learn that marriage is an endless lesson for couples to learn from each other and reconcile needs and wants in an intertwined vision for the relationship to develop and develop?

Identify marital problems

Most marriages fail because couples do not recognise some marital issues. Most of us tend to ignore the challenge, believing that everything will happen. But they do not understand that identifying the first signs of marital problems can be of great help in solving these problems. Dealing with the fact that there is no perfect marriage or relationship is an excellent way to start. The union, however perfect the picture may be, will at some point work on rocky paths. What we might consider as simple problems, such as a trip on the highway, paying bills, forgetting a promise and overtime can be severe for our partner. Often the root cause of all fervent arguments is the inability of another person to admit their mistake. Married couples only have the opportunity to recognise the challenges of marriage positively and to work together to make a marriage successful. It is a well-known fact that complacency only indicates marital disputes, which in turn can lead to divorce.

Seek professional help
Strangely, seeking professional advice can help a lot in getting married. Marriage counselling and couple therapy should not be treated as a last resort to save your relationship. From time to time, by evaluating each couple's ideas and providing good marriage advice to a counsellor or occupational therapist,

husbands and wives gain a clearer perspective on what to expect and what to expect. 'they can do to improve their relationship. Often, we are embarrassed to consult with advisers about the familiar concept of a society fueled by scandals, because by doing so, you are acknowledging that your relationship is falling apart. But don't let this concept keep you and your partner from trying to understand better how your marriage works.

To bring back love

Professional help, such as couple therapy, can be beneficial, but the development of unstable relationships should not stop. Bring romance and intimacy to your wedding as you pass through days of exciting dating again. Rekindle the calluses of love, covered with a lot of frustration, conflict and communication gaps. Make way for exciting surprises, spend time alone, go on vacation and dine for two, etc.

Advice on rational therapy of emotional behaviour.

Albert Ellis developed Rational Emotional Behavioral Therapy (REBT). This short, direct and targeted therapy focuses on solving specific problems that affect a person or, in the case of relationship counselling, a couple in distress. The basic principle of REBT is that our emotions come only from our beliefs, not from events that occur in our lives. Like this, it is of most extreme significance that our convictions are stable and balanced because the results of these convictions will be enthusiastic development and satisfaction. On the no chance that our opinions are silly and pointless, our passionate lives experience the ill effects of hypochondrias, for example, self-trickery, melancholy and tension. REBT is an instructive procedure in which the advisor shows the customer how to recognise unreasonable convictions, challenge them and replace them with other rational beliefs. In relationship counselling, once the married couple has strong opinions, the emotional difficulties and problematic behaviours cease.

Ellis believed that human beings were born with a double potential for healthy and unhealthy thought processes. He called rational thinking rational process, and sick diversity was irrational thinking. Logical thinking, as you would expect, means an objective view of things as they are, while irrational thinking distorts reality by misinterpreting things that happen.

At the centre of REBT is the A-B-C personality theory. A represents an activation event, usually a type of stressful life situation. An example of activation could be a teenager who was kicked out by his girlfriend. B represents a conviction that dominates and causes emotional consequences, represented by C. If the belief is irrational (for example, the child believes that "I am the loser"), the result is probably depression or anger. Alternatively, if the belief is rational (for example, "I am a precious person"), the consequence would be only temporary sadness upon disconnection. Crucial for Ellis is that believing, not triggering events, has emotional effects. Therefore, if a person has a variety of irrational beliefs, they are likely to experience a lot of emotional pain throughout their life with different challenges. Whereas, if a person's feelings are rational, then they can face a disappointing life event with balance. In other words, the way you feel is mainly determined by the way you think.

Where do our irrational beliefs come from? Ellis learned that we learn some of them from other people during childhood and do the rest ourselves. This is the only way Ellis cared about the past: we learn from our current beliefs from past encounters. The past can't be changed, and REBT places little emphasis on its discussion; Instead, REBT strives to replace illogical beliefs with logical beliefs.

In Ellis' thought, silly convictions are the reason for human hypochondrias, including discouragement and tension. Nonsensical convictions will in general disregard the positive, overstate the negative, misshape reality or potentially over-generalise. REBT teaches that people tend to exaggerate with "musts", "musts" and "oils". Many of these self-critical beliefs are brainwashed at the start of life and are reinforced as the person examines them.

What are the irrational beliefs most frequently discussed in relationship counselling? You probably see one of them "my partner should do what I think he should do". Another irrational belief that is often seen in relationship counselling is, "I need my partner's approval."

As mentioned above, according to the theory of personality A-B-C, beliefs, which do not trigger events, cause emotional consequences. When the feeling is irrational, emotion is not healthy. The effects of irrational beliefs can be relatively mild (like procrastination) but can also be very damaging, immobilizing or even dangerous.

Ellis learned that unconditional self-acceptance and acceptance of the other is absolute in the pursuit of well-being. Healthy people know they are not perfect and will continue to make mistakes, but they still consider themselves worthy. They are only regarded as precious because they are alive; in fact, they enjoy life and have the opportunity to experience it regularly. In the case of relationship counselling, it is essential to accept the other (partner) as well as to accept yourself unconditionally.

Recalling the theory of personality A-B-C, successful advice on REBT relationships adds steps D, E and F.D is a dispute: the therapist helps the married couple to cope with the irrational belief (B). Ellis suggested that the therapist ask the married couple if there was evidence of an idea or what would be the worst possible outcome if the couple gave up that belief. In therapy, a relationship counsellor can report misconceptions, but he also teaches clients how to challenge them in their daily lives outside of therapy. The result of challenging self-destructive beliefs and replacing them with rational expectations creates a practical philosophy

(E) as well as a new set of feelings (F) that do not weaken.

Although the REBT teaches that the counsellor must demonstrate complete unconditional acceptance, the therapist is not encouraged to establish a warm and caring relationship with the client. The only task of a relationship counsellor is to help the married couple to identify and confront irrational beliefs and replace them with rational expectations. Therapists are generally not at all interested in past events that are the source of an irrational belief; All that matters is the removal of this belief in the present.

Successful collaboration in counselling for relationships between REBT therapists and partners results in changes in the knowledge of both individuals. As a result, both parties feel better about themselves and the other. Self-destructive thinking stops and behavioural changes occur. Both partners move towards unconditional self-acceptance and unconditional acceptance of the other.

Relational therapy and attachment style
Maybe these are things that have been bitten by a snake, but relationships only relate to the nature of relationships. At the point when you begin to look all starry eyed at, your nervous system science is flooded with brain chemicals (neurotransmitters) that make you feel love, joy and ecstasy. Each of you feels that you have met a soul mate and that you can only see her beauty and wonder, again, she is a great person! When both brains swim in exaggerated neurotransmitters, the connection is ideal. Over time, these chemicals in your mind return to normal, but if you have a stable relationship, the transition from "falling in love" to "falling in love" begins. This phase is really about staying "connected" and feeling secure. Psychologically, we all have a connection style, or more precisely, an "attachment style". The study documented four styles of connection or connection: safe, anxious, avoidant and fearless.

The first group is defined as insurance. This means that these people expect their partners to be there for them, to be adaptable and to meet their needs. They can seek love and care when they need it. They are also attentive and attentive to their partners when necessary. They believe things will get better. They readily share their feelings and receive the opinions of their partners with curiosity and respect.

The people concerned generally fear that the relationship is not at best secure. They are psychologically and physiologically disturbed when there is a real or perceived threat to the link (i.e. your partner did not call when you said you would; your partner was preoccupied with the tasks, not by their involvement). They may not feel secure when they share their needs because they do not expect to be served and will not respond. This uncertainty in relationships leads to behaviours that can alienate partners, thus creating insecurity that worries them. Sometimes these behaviours inspire the couple to distance themselves, increasing their anxiety.

Also, avoid making people feel insecure about relationships, but show insecurity differently. In response to concerns that the demands of relationships are beyond their means, they withdraw and mentally diminish the feeling of need for a relationship. These are people who say they need "space". And they indeed need space, but too often, in this "space", they reduce the feeling of love and pleasure of the couple by focusing on their faults. Withdrawals seem cold and do not affect termination, but physiological measurements show that they are also at risk, similar to those in the disturbed category. These are people who, after having broken up with a partner, remember that this person was a perfect couple and may even regret having broken off their relationship. They feel alone again and want to be in a relationship. Chances are you can see the challenges that anxious and avoidant people would face. Some die of fear, others flee. It is a familiar dynamic that can lead to frustration if it is not understood and successfully dealt with.

A person who is afraid of being avoided has usually survived some trauma. They are prone to relationships, but at the same time, they are terrified because people have been brought up and abused in the past. They are more reactive to troubles, real or imagined, relationships and can protest dramatically. Withdrawals and anxious routines can alternate.

Appendix of your style

We quickly review the complex literature on attachment styles. Your connection style and your accomplice's connection style will significantly affect how they interact with each other. Most importantly, his methods will inform you emotionally (no matter what is said intellectually), how secure or insecure you feel through the ups and downs of life and connection. Romantic relationships inspire and expire. There are times when love and connection flow. There are times when passion and connection become obsessed.

Conflicts also arise. Two people in safety tolerate this downpour and this flow and navigate through conflicts. They understand that love lasts, even in times of disappointment, discord or temporary separation (that is, the request to take a child or exercise). Lovers, fear avoiders, and fear avoiders find it harder to manage, and their interactions often become "protests" against their experience of threatening relationships: too little, too much, too unpredictable.

Here's the point: whatever the fight or the debate, I've found that the essence of it all is to feel connected. The accompanying segment clarifies in more detail how this bottom line is often lost in the patterns that emerge. Along the way, the starting group is disproportionately charged with anxious and dishonest people. Safe people go out together from the evacuation pool.

The contents

The distinction between "content" and "process" is sometimes a difficult concept. They seem to be words that therapists throw away and make little sense of, but in reality, they mean a lot. "Content" is a thing, a theme or a theme. The "process" is his way, his way, it says. The content would be something like this movie to watch Batman or The Miserables. The process would be how you communicated with your partner on the video to watch. ("The last time you chose the movie! Now it's my turn" or "Let's keep watching until we find the one we like"). The process often becomes a complicated model to identify and modify.

In my experience, couples often come to therapy trapped in content. They debate who did what, who said what, mostly struggling with content. They don't think the problem is the struggle process itself, and they miss that the result, the connection, is usually the real problem. In any case, when individuals have contrasts, it's conceivable to discover a relationship. Still, if you focus on the content (rather than the process and the connection), you can quickly feel disengaged. Furthermore, when you feel detached, particularly over a significant stretch, love collapses and relationships can be in trouble.

Ask a real question

Like the iceberg, "content" is the tip, and the "real problem" is most of the subsurface that a ship can sink. It is essential to know what is beneath the surface and to deal with it directly and effectively. I worked with a married couple where one person was agitated by the violent nature of their partner at parties. The content, expressed in the form of criticism, was that the partner was too naughty, which made others also interested in him. While I was talking to them, I had a photo showing that the person in question was a "pit bull", watching carefully and occasionally howling strangers approaching them. I told this person that they may not need to be as "alert" (it was clear to me that their partner was very loyal). I said the other person that she would occasionally register to convince her partner that he or she was at a party, even when it was nice to meet new people at a party. The real problem here is the feeling of insecurity in the relationship (something that one of these people naturally suffered because of the infidelity in a previous relationship). Another real problem here is the need for another partner to understand the history of his partner better and to be attentive and sensitive to his feelings (qualities of secure attachment).

Another thing that happens when the real problem is not recognised and the couple closes in the content trap is escalation. When people are not heard, they repeat and speak louder. It's almost a fact. When you focus on content ("always forget to take out the trash"), your partner is likely to become defensive, which prevents him from being heard. Then loud voices or other examples (content) arrive on the scene. (I admit that it happened to your friends a lot more than you did). For this example, reviewing the garbage disposal all the time causes a couple to argue. The real problem (that is, I don't think you care, which can be based on waste-free experiences) remains unresolved, and the "negative loop" can get out of hand, causing damage and is also a way to understand why a partner has not engaged in a "past disappointment". Most likely, the real problem beneath the surface has not been adequately resolved.

Change the pattern

The job of couple therapy is to go beyond the "content" and change the "scheme". Content comes and goes, but when the process or form works, whatever it is, it can be managed, and a successful model pays attention to the connection. The first step is to look at the "content trap" and the next "negative loop" as the enemy, not your partner. Your partner is not the enemy! The enemy is the content trap and the subsequent negative loop. It's essential

The next step is to learn new and effective ways to communicate. One of the couple I worked with shared their feelings (something legitimate and essential to do) was the same as sharing "theories" about their partner (that is, "I feel like you're cheating on me!") Explaining that they are the feelings and theories of different things were helpful to both. To say "I feel insecure and I need security" is very different from the words: "I have the impression that you are lying to me, that you have something that I do not know about person" x ", etc." Part of its form was accusations of harmful intent and behaviour, which were exchanged for angry, defensive rejections which led to a "negative cycle" which exacerbated the pain, sadness and disconnection. Until they got to the right problem (uncertainty) and found ways to resolve it directly, speaking clearly and strengthening their sense of security, nothing worked. Now this couple can talk about feelings without theories faster, listen and respond to the needs of others, and reconnect. What did we say? That's right, the connection.

The importance of performance

John Gottman, PhD Sc. He writes a lot on relationship issues, and I highly recommend his books. One of the things he has discovered in more than 30 years of research into what makes relationships happy and lasting is accessories. If there is a 5: 1 relationship of mutual interactions with negative/complicated interactions, couples describe their relationships as comfortable and inclined to stay together, no matter how much they argue.

It's simple! Think how nice it is, how connected you are with your partner when you are the recipient or donor of the supplement. There are things you like about your partner and the things he wants about you. If you can focus on these things on purpose and, more importantly, complement your partner with what you notice, you will create a happier relationship. Statements that start with "really appreciate" or "thanks for" or "you're always good at" are great ways to add a fraction of the report that should be "5". This is a piece of what adds to a safe relationship, the feeling that although there are problems and failures in our partner and us, the overall experience is pleasant and expected in the future.

Inadequate marriage therapy is worse than staying at home and watching TV

All the couples who came to see me after trying marriage therapy were amazed at the simplicity of a good marriage. The psychological community doesn't need to give marriage counselling. Their area is that of mental illness, and they help those who are psychologically disabled. People traumatized by an event often need the help of a psychologist. But those who have difficulty getting married do not need "marital therapy".

A somewhat strange thought. How to deal with marriage? It may make sense to receive individual therapy after a divorce, but that's it. A bad marriage is not a psychological problem.

The only marital therapy you need for a bad marriage is called "education."

Marriage is fundamentally a spiritual concept of fusion of two souls to regulate procreation (for material life), to develop a friendship (for spirit) and to learn to love each other unconditionally (for the soul). If you and your spouse are undergoing joint therapy, you will learn techniques that drain the rest of your relationship; Such is the devastating power of his strange methods.

Education is the key to saving marriages. When couples learn the dynamic construction of friendship and learn the principles on which marriage is based, they can make it work. Sometimes it will take a bit of encouragement, but usually, the fear of failure and the potential for so much joy are quite exhilarating. A well-understood and well-functioning marriage are lovely, and the little effort it takes to change is just a small salary.

A bad marriage can end immediately.

The actions of the couple measure the difference between a bad and good marriage

When you want to have a good marriage, all you have to do is stop the wrong words, thoughts and actions. It's that simple! If you ignore the distorted explanations given by those who provide the so-called marital therapy, everything will be fine (when you know what to say, think and do).

Imagine a time when you stand on a cliff and collapse because you are so close to the edge. But then you look outside and see the beautiful ocean and the colourful sky. Just as your fear and despair have turned into joy, it's the same with your marriage. You have to change your perspective and your expectations of failure and fear of success; it depends entirely on you!

Examine what I am saying. Watch your mind for a few seconds. Listen to the feelings of fear as if it were not your words, but your thoughts. Take a step back and say to the mind that everything is fine and everything will be fine. Have you noticed that you just sighed? You have a lot more control than you think. You need to learn what you need to control and how to control it. You have to learn what makes you happy and how to do it. He must learn to treat his wife and to open his heart.

Chapter 5: The Communication Conundrum

Communication is absolutely necessary for your relationship to thrive. Without it, the love and fire in your relationship will grow cold and dead. Communication is like oxygen to a relationship. Most people think effective communication is all about merely listening actively, but there is so much more to it. It would also behoove you to realize that each gender communicates, differently because they see things differently.

Thanks to the science of psychology, we understand that the differences in communication between the genders are partly as a result of both genders being kept apart from each other while growing up. Since girls mostly hang out with girls and boys with boys due to societal norms and cultures, there can be a bit of disconnect in understanding the way the other gender processes stuff and communicates how they feel. It's almost always a case of little boys playing with trucks and little girls playing dress up or dolls.

Communication Isn't Just Verbal

Communication is not only verbal, however. It is also important to understand that non-verbal cues differ for both men and women. Of course the facial expressions for a lot of situations will remain the same. Like the typical grimace when anyone, male or female, bites into a slice of lemon, as opposed to the smile that follows a bite of homemade lemon meringue pie.

There are seven types of non-verbal cues. Knowing how both genders use these cues will change the way you and your spouse communicate with each other for the better. This way, you can become more aware of your lover's goals, hopes, needs, and fears, with little or no misunderstanding. Let's take a look at what these non-verbal cues are.

Physical contact: Regardless of genetic makeup, males and females communicate very differently through touch. While for men heavy slaps on the back and rough nudges are a way to display camaraderie, power, influence, and dominance, women take the much gentler route of offering a hug or reaching out to pat the other person's shoulder to show compassion, or simply refraining from touch when not in the mood or angry or wronged in some way.

Thanks to science and a whole lot of research, we now know that touch causes the release of oxytocin, which automatically causes the couple sharing the touch to feel better about themselves and in one another's company, no matter how terrible their days have gone. Sometimes it is not Advil you need, but a great big hug.

Facial expressions: The human face is a wonder. There are 43 different facial muscles in the face, which are capable of a myriad of expressions — the closest and most recent estimate being approximately 10,000. This makes human facial expression one of the most important non-verbal ways we communicate.

More often than not, women use a lot of facial expressions. There is eye contact, or the lack of it. There's nodding the head, and pursing of the lips — a lot more compared to men. In addition to having a lot of facial expressions, women are often better at reading facial expressions, thanks to their intuitive and evocative nature. If you doubt this, try telling a lie to a female. For the most part, it won't take long until you're found out.

Paralinguistic communication: Have you ever wondered why a word or sentence can imply several different things depending on the way it's said? If you have, then you either know of or have had some experience with a little something called **paralinguistic communication.**

Also called "para language," it is the study of voice, tone, and the various nuances and cues accompanying words when they are said. They represent aspects of communication that go beyond words. There are a bunch of things to consider when we speak of paralanguage, including fluency, pitch, accent, speech rate, and modulation. You've also got to keep track of cues like hand gestures, body language, eye movements, and the like.

Paralinguistic communication is important, as the more you understand it, the less likely people will be able to hide the truth and cover up emotions around you. This is a great thing, because once you know what the actual problem you're addressing with your spouse at any given point in time is, it's easier for you to address the actual issue, and not the secondary reason they give you.

Body posture: Since men usually tend to command more personal space than the female folk, they are more likely to align their bodies in a such a way that their feet are more spaced apart, with their arms placed farther apart from their bodies when they are upset or feel challenged. Females, on the other hand, retract and keep their arms close together with their feet crossed when they feel intimidated, afraid, or averse to a particular person or situation.

You want to be careful when you're interpreting body language. Always pay attention to the context in which you observe it. Don't assume your wife is upset with you because she's hugging herself — it could just be really cold outside for her.

Causes of Miscommunication in a Relationship

The he versus she complex: While women use communication as a means to build relationships and intimacy, men don't understand the logic behind using so many words. Many men are of the opinion that communication should have a clear goal and they see no use communicating if they are not allowed to fix anything.

If a woman tells her spouse about how she feels overweight and finds it difficult to lose the post baby weight, a typical male response would probably be along the lines of, "I have the number of a great personal trainer," or "Why don't you cut down on all those fries?" Now these comments may sound like an insult to her body image, but he genuinely feels he is offering advice. All the woman wants is to be told she is beautiful no matter what the scale reads.

Active or passive listening? It is a Herculean task to get most men to listen without wanting to chip in with a solution or their feelings about an issue. Another issue would probably be just how much to say in a given situation. Just how much is too much? Before a man answers a question or narrates an occurrence, he has sifted through the events in his own mind. In the end, he only winds up telling the aspects he feels are connected to the story.

The reverse is the case with the opposite gender. Women use the power of words to fully comprehend their experiences and emotions. There are times when a woman may not understand what she is feeling and why she feels that way, until after she has talked about it. This is why the worst thing you could possibly do is not respond when a woman is sharing her feelings and thoughts with you. You may assume you're paying attention and that should be enough, but that's not the case. You should show that you do indeed understand her, by putting yourself in her shoes and feeling what she feels, too.

These differences in communication would explain why a man becomes withdrawn and retreats to a spot where he feels safest (man cave, anyone?) This man cave serves as a mini vacation spot without the extra expenses incurred with tickets and such. In the safety of his own space, he sorts out his emotions, and tries to comprehend what he is feeling.

This period of withdrawal can leave his spouse wondering if she is at fault in some way or if she is losing him. That's not necessarily the case. Women, when confronted with a particularly tight or difficult situation, would value support and some level of care and nurturing from her significant other, as she would definitely use words to communicate and try to process her feelings.

Avoiding Misunderstandings

Now that the complex nature of communication has been established, and I have made it clear that gender differences only add to this complexity, I want to point out that all this does not mean men and women are incapable of getting along. They can. It's simply a matter of practice, and a willingness to understand one another.

The overall purpose of improving communication in your relationship or marriage is to adapt to one another's style of communication, rather than try to change the other person completely. Here are some facts you need to be aware of if you want to practice effective communication with your significant other:

Recognise that communication has different and distinct styles and each have their strengths and weaknesses.

Understand these and don't be quick to find faults or point accusing fingers.

Try not to fit into or feed the stereotypes that exists with gender differences. Understand that the environment plays a huge part in the way to respond verbally or nonverbally.

Be aware and get information concerning the different communication styles in order to effectively control your response to each one. Recognise the different styles that exist, and adapt fluidly to each one.

Chapter 6: Perception And Shared Experience

Does it Take Two to Tango?

Chances are this is not the first material you've ever read on how to improve your relationship and chances are some of the other stuff you've read has helped at least in the short run. Those books and articles probably gave you some valuable insights into how your difficulties arose, and some useful tips for handling conflict, improving communication, and enhancing intimacy and yet you probably found that in the long run, not that much really seemed to change. You soon fell back into old habits, the same old issues reared their ugly heads, and those communication skills just didn't seem to work as well in real life as they did in the transcriptions in the book.

I know this all very well from my own encounter. I am an avid consumer of self-help books, I never thought I'd one day be writing my own and I have gone through these cycles myself, over and over. Many books and articles on relationships have a strong focus on skills and techniques like these:

Influencing your partner via effective negotiation, communication, assertiveness, and conflict-resolution skills

Creating rituals and developing activities to cultivate affection, warmth, fun, sensuality, sexuality, intimacy, and so on

Developing insight into the differences between you and your partner, and how they have arisen as a result of your different backgrounds

All of these are important and useful, and we will certainly touch on them within these pages. However, notice that these themes are all focused on areas of life that are out of your direct control. For example, even if you mastered all the known skills on the planet for influencing others' behavior, you still could not control them. Sorry, but there is just no guarantee that they will respond to your masterful communication, assertiveness, and negotiation skills in the way that you would like. Similarly creating rituals and

91

developing shared activities is of vital importance for a healthy relationship, but here again it requires your partner's cooperation; therefore it is not in your direct control. So, when you come to address this very important issue with your partner, here's what you will find: either he will cooperate or he won't. There's no method you can force him to cooperate; you can only ask. Last but not least, developing insight into your differences is very useful: it enhances your own self-awareness and helps you to understand how your partner operates. But once again, it involves focusing on something outside your control; you can't alter those differences between the two of you, and you can't change the life history that has led to them.

So, while we will address these important topics, they will not be the main subject matter in this book. Our aim in ACT is to help you make the most of your life and the more you learn to focus on what is in your control, the more empowerment and fulfillment you will experience. In contrast, the more you focus on what is out of your control, the more you will feel disempowered, dissatisfied, and disappointed. This is a fact in our life that we all readily forget, so I'll be reminding you of it repeatedly throughout this book.

The bulk of this book will consist of looking at these topics:

How to stop doing things that make your relationship worse

How to simplify and react on your worth and to be closer to the person you ideally like to be

How to take up what you can't control

How to successfully handle the painful feelings and stressful thoughts that inevitably occur in every relationship

Notice that these things are all under your direct control. You can choose to stop doing things that drain your relationship regardless of what your partner does. You can likely choose to be similar to your partner regardless of what your partner does. You can choose to accept what you can't control rather than dwelling on it or struggling with it in ways that suck the life out of you and your relationship. And once you learn how to effectively handle the stress and pain your relationship brings, you can choose how to answer when the going gets tough, which it will.

You are likely to discover a great paradox here: as you shift your focus to these areas that are within your direct control, you will often find your partner starts to make definite changes instantly without you even asking her. No guarantee of that, of course. But it does very often happen, and it makes perfect sense when you think about it. Imagine spending a lot of time with someone who is constantly complaining, criticizing, finding fault, pointing out the problems, and dwelling on the difficulties in your relationship and then, all of a sudden, he changes. Suddenly she becomes a lot easier to be around. He becomes open, warm, easygoing, and willing to put all differences aside. Wouldn't you start to act differently toward a partner like this? Wouldn't your behavior change in positive ways?

Of course, this doesn't mean letting your partner walk all over you or have her way all the time. There needs to be a stability of give and take in order to keep a relationship healthy and meaningful. So of course, it does take two to tango. However, if you practice the dance steps alone, then the next time you dance with your partner, it will go more smoothly.

Reality Check

At this point, it's time for a reality check: no two partners will make changes to exactly the same extent. One is almost always more motivated than the other. If you cannot make room for this reality, then you will turn it into yet another problem to keep you stuck in the rut. "That's all very well," I hear you say, "but what happens if I do all the hard work, and he makes no effort at all?" Well, if this happens, your relationship is still likely to improve, but obviously it will be a long way off reaching its full potential. So, if that's what ultimately happens, then you will need to make a difficult choice: to stay or leave. But if you do choose to leave at that point, then at least you know you gave it a good try and furthermore, you will have experienced some valuable personal growth and developed some skills that will help you in other relationships with your friends, family, coworkers, and any future partner. Nevertheless, if neither of you do any work, then your relationship is guaranteed to go from bad to worse.

Chapter 7: Communication For Avoiding Fights

There are several ways to communicate with your spouse without offending their feelings or increasing arguments. One can remain assertive and put their point across in a more non-offensive and effective manner by using a series of highly proven communication tactics. Though communication styles can vary, the ultimate goal should convey your point in a more convincing and persuasive manner to avoid hurting the other person's feelings and to prevent any potential misunderstandings.

Here are some tips that will help you avoid fights or communicate without getting offensive.

1. Know the Other Person's Perspective

Almost always, there are two sides to every story. Likewise, any disagreement has two distinct angles. It can simply be a matter of perspective. Your partner may be seeing things in a different way from you, and unless you are open to hearing their perspective, you won't know what they are thinking or how they are seeing things. Listen, and understand their perspective rather than staunchly believing that yours is the only right way of thinking.

Show genuine interest in understanding them even though you may not necessarily agree with them. Many times, we may not agree with what our spouse says or believes. However, it doesn't mean we shouldn't lend them a patient hearing or at least understand where they are coming from.

For example, your spouse may appear to be over possessive, jealous and suspicious about you all the time, which you may not agree with or accept. In your eyes, you've done nothing to trigger suspicion or possessiveness. However, the spouse may have been cheated in past relationships, and are therefore unable to get over the feeling. This may have made them increasingly jealous, possessive and suspicious in all relationships. Of course, you don't have to live with your spouse's past baggage, and it can be highly annoying.

However, that doesn't mean you shouldn't show understanding or concern towards them. Understand where they are coming from even if you may not appreciate it. Grab opportunities to get them to talk, and listen to their perspectives. You may gain insights you hadn't otherwise considered. The explanation or flow of conversation may hold points that you had otherwise missed.

One of the guaranteed ways to avoid hurting others is putting yourself in their shoes. Imagine things from their perspective. How would you feel if you were in their place and he/she would talk to you the way you are talking to them? Wouldn't you be hurt and upset? Practice imagining or visualizing how the other person feels when you say or do certain hurtful things. Just because someone's opinion doesn't match yours, doesn't mean they are wrong.

2. Control Your Verbal and Non-Verbal Body Language

Be cautious with your honestly and straightforwardness at times. You want to be truthful and communicate your feelings, yes. However, truth should also be accompanied by compassion and kindness. Don't take potshots at their dreams or ideas. Even if you think something isn't going to work, tell them in a kinder way. For example, your spouse may come up with a business plan that you know isn't feasible in reality. Keep your words and actions in check.

Instead of making fun of the plan of their ideas, sit with them and talk to them about how it can be much better if they put in some time, effort and thought into it. You want to be honest rather than mislead them, but you also want to do in a manner that isn't hurtful. Don't grimace or use offensive/derogatory words. Never get personal or rake up past issues in the present argument.

Sometimes, the mere tone of your voice is enough to send people in another direction or convey your disappointment or disapproval. Unlike our words, the voice tone is more subconsciously guided. This means that our feelings, thoughts, and emotions are evident through the voice even though words can be manipulated in a certain manner. Try to talk with a more neutral tone if you don't want to communicate your feelings or wish you keep them in control.

Once you have already expressed your disagreement or disappointment verbally to your spouse, there is no need to back it up with non-verbal actions too. Once you've made your point, avoid repeating it or using other forms of communication to convey the same point once you've driven it home effectively.

It can only end up hurting your cause as constantly telling a person something potentially offensive makes them feel like you're accusing them and puts them on the defensive.

3. Construct Your Sentences as Opinions and Not Facts

When you are telling your spouse something that can be potentially offensive or hurtful, don't put it across as the ultimate gospel truth or fact! Facts work for people who have a more open and liberal perspective. However, it may seem accusatory or similar to personal attacks for people who are not open to understanding a different point of view. Don't force your perspective as the only truth. Avoid criticizing, demonizing or condemning people.

Instead of using statements such as, "you are absolutely wrong", try something like, "I think you may not be right there." You are stating it as a perspective or opinion instead of brandishing judgments. You can also agree with their justification or perspective if the two are consistent. This reveals that your statement is not directly addressed to them in a hateful manner or to get back to them. Avoid exaggerating reality. Don't use words such as "never" or "always." In the heat of the moment, we use idioms and phrases that stretch the truth. Don't resort to hype roles, stick to honesty. Don't allow your emotions to speed up.

Take a deep breath and get a good grip of your emotions before you take off on your spouse. I know people, who in a bid to control or manage their emotions more effectively; take some time off to cool down before speaking to their partner. A cooling off period ensures that you are not making the heat of the moment statements or accusations. You also more time to keep your body language and non-verbal clues in check.

4. Don't Take Disagreements Personally

Being honest and being right are two different things. You can be wrong and honest for all you know. Just because someone is stating their point honestly doesn't make them right. Similarly, you can be right, honest, and end up hurting your spouse's feelings. Be genuine about your perspective but if your spouse disagrees with it, don't take it personally. There may be a perspective or justification for their disagreement.

Resist the urge to transform their perspective to match yours. Just listen and absorb what they are trying to communicate. They have the right to their opinion and honesty just as you had a right to yours. Value your opinion, point of view and perspective. Even if you don't disagree verbally or vociferously, remember your opinion is valid. You have as much right, to be honest about your perspective as the other person.

If you offer an honest perspective, and your spouse isn't open to hearing from you, pushing the issue will only make matters worse and create hurtful feelings. He or she may not be ready for agreeing with you. Avoid succumbing to the temptation of getting the other person to agree with everything you are saying. Sometimes, people should be allowed to make their mistakes. Also, if they don't agree with you, it doesn't make you wrong. It just means the person has a different perspective, which you shouldn't take too personally.

Tips for Diffusing Arguments with Your Partner

Arguments are an inescapable part of married life. If a couple says they never argue about anything, chances are they are lying. When two distinct individuals are involved, there are bound to be differences. There are heated discussions with people we truly care about or those we are close to. This is naturally true for our spouse too. Arguments may not be avoidable. However, not letting things snowball or get bigger is completely within our realm of control.

If you are drawn into a verbal altercation, use the following tips for defusing the argument and returning to a place of calmness and tranquility, where differences can be discussed in a healthier and rational manner.

1. Pick Your Battles

In a perfect world, all arguments will end with both parties agreeing to each other's perspective and moving away in a fulfilled and positive manner. However, the reality is far different than the perfect couple kingdom we dream of building. Differences don't automatically evaporate in thin air. The key to conflict management is learning to identify a lost cause. Pick your battles wisely. Know when it's not going to be worth it to put up a good fight. Look at the overall good rather than holding on to your viewpoint in a stubborn manner. If budging slightly is going to save you time and plenty of heartaches, it may be worth it.

For instance, several happy and wise couples learn that there are plenty of topics that shouldn't be discussed between them such as politics or relatives (potentially acrimonious topics). Understand that there are topics, where differences will always exist. It is sensible to avoid these topics.

2. Calm Down

Even minor arguments can snowball into large issues if they aren't tackled or nipped in the bud. If both you and your spouse let a minor issue blow up into something huge by letting your emotions get the better of you, there's going to be nothing but fights. Damaging words can cause irreparable damage to the relationship, which you or your spouse may later regret. Avoid letting your emotions get the better of you in any situation, and stay as calm as possible.

Practice anger management hacks such as deep breathing or counting up to 20. Take a break from the argument if you think it is on the verge of becoming more intense. Go for a walk, give it some time, and come back with a fresh perspective. Avoid all this by being calm. Each time you find your anger rising, do something relaxing, therapeutic and stress-busting before going back into the discussion. It won't just reduce your anger but also give you greater clarity of perspective. Sometimes, when you give it time, you'll realize that you hadn't really seen it from the other person's point of view.

3. Stick Only To the Topic

A healthy argument is always to the point and non-personal. There's no place for raking up past issues or hitting below the belt on matters that are totally unconnected or irrelevant to the topic of argument. If you use personal insults or hit at the other person's character, it reveals a lot about yours. When we are seething with rage, it is easy to lose perspective or broaden the scope of our fight. The dispute or difference becomes a scope to settle scores or get even with your partner by using a variety of attacks.

This annoyance invariably includes all topics under the sun, including unfortunate personal attacks, which make matters worse. For example, you may start fighting about the fact that it is always you who is doing all household chores, while your partner watches television or plays virtual games. This doesn't mean you can tell him or her about how everyone in his or her family is lazy, low on ambition and good for nothing. They may in return be shocked about how you are belittling their family and may say it to you.

To which, you will go on to reply that exactly 6 days, an hour and 36 seconds ago, he or she had said demeaning things about your family too. What you are doing is using a real current issue (not contributing towards household chores) for settling earlier scores. This doesn't resolve your current issue and makes past grudges even worse. Don't use a small argument about doing the laundry as a full-blown excuse for lashing out at your better half's character.

If you must squabble, keep it related to the issue at hand. Focus on the present issue rather playing 'ten weeks ago you did so and so now I am getting even' game. This will lead to more hurt and pain, and the original matter still remains unresolved. Focus on the issue at hand, and work out a middle way to tackle the conflict so you arrive at a more peaceful outcome. The more you and your spouse stick to specific details of an issue, the higher are your chances of resolving it in a more peaceful manner.

4. Watch Your Body Language, Tone and Mannerisms

Hurtful and destructive confrontations comprise a bunch of painful and hurting insults that are hurled back and forth.

Shouting at the top of your voice, displaying aggressiveness through body language, keeping a more standoffish stance, raising your tone and more are all signs of harshness. Sometimes, even without noticing or knowing if we come across as highly hostile.

Of course, you can see yourself in the mirror otherwise you'll know how hostile you look. Sometimes, while talking a person will slowly raise their tone unknowingly and demonstrate their rage-filled feelings! Speak in a more gentle, calm, polite and neutral manner. This will make you come across as more assertive, and people will listen to you. Rather than screaming and yelling, talk to people in a more assertive, calm and confident tone. Irrespective of the nature of the discussion, keeping a friendly disposition and attitude will ensure that the conflict doesn't escalate.

5. Accept Your Differences

In an ideal world, all arguments will end with both partners settling their differences and agreeing with each other's perspective and walking away into the sunset holding hands. Reality and expectations are diverse worlds though. For god's sake, you are a couple not a pair of Siamese twins. Have you ever wondered how boring life will be if your spouse is exactly like you? There will be differences. However, these differences are the basis of making your relationship more exciting.

It's a good complement when you and your spouse combine forces to create a stellar relationship. Spouses needn't always think or be alike. Their differences can be a good complement to each other. Married life and communication become easier once you accept that there will be differences, and consciously work on these differences.

You and your spouse may have grown up in different environments with a different set of values and upbringing, which may have led to the development of a unique personality or beliefs. Don't get into a relationship with the notion that just because you both are a couple; you should be alike in all aspects.

Yes, you may have to be on the same thought process when it comes to joint decisions, say raising children, managing the house and taking care of finances. However, it isn't necessary to be alike in everything. Learn to respect and celebrate each other's differences to enjoy a happier and fulfilling relationship.

Chapter 8: Top Relationship-Strengthening Activities For Couples

When it comes to relationship issues, sometimes a couple is unable to note that there is a problem that may jeopardize dynamics and functionality of their relationship until the problem becomes evolved to the point where it appears to be drawing only more problems. That is why it is likewise important to work on preventing these issues, which is most efficiently done with relationship-strengthening activities for couples. There is always more room for improvement, while your relationship should flourish as long as you are ready to make an effort and commit.

"Pillow Talks"

We can't emphasize enough how important clear communication in relationships is. That is why our first relationship-strengthening activity on the list is dedicated to encouraging communication between couples. One of the best ways of practicing communication is to start with casual and "carefree" talk sessions. If you are used to spending the evening alone but together – you may continue to read that book you started with several days ago and your partner is hooked to the TV or smartphone – you may decide to disconnect from lonesome activities and shut off the world, while you focus on each other. You may lay down in bed or settle down on the sofa, it doesn't matter which location you choose – what matters is that you are not alone together. Start talking about your day, about your plans, start a conversation on anything that crosses your mind. Pillow talk topics may also revolve around affectionate talk, which is a great way of showing appreciation for your partner through verbal and non-verbal communication. Cuddling is also allowed as you are talking, sharing opinions and focusing on what the other has to say. This exercise is due to help you establish or reestablish connection with your partner, while practicing openness, communication, appreciation and intimacy. Once you make these "pillow talks" your and your partner's routine, you might be surprised by how many new things you and your partner have found out about your each other.

Mutual Interests and Hobbies

Although you and your partner may be different when it comes to preferences and characteristics, you surely have some things in common. In case you start tracing similarities between your partner and yourself, you may be surprised with how many things you actually have in common. Everything you and your partner have in common can be used as an advantage in the process of improving your relationship. One of the best ways of strengthening your relationship is to find activities and hobbies that suit your mutual interests and focus on connecting through these activities. Instead of focusing on the ways you are different from one another, you should place an emphasis on similarities that can serve the purpose of helping you reconnect with your partner, while taking advantage of spending more time together through shared activities and hobbies.

"Who Are You?"

In the beginning of every relationship, your partner appears to be a perfect match and everything you feel and see speaks in favor of the idea that you have found an ideal partner. As time is passing by, you are getting to know each other better, so both you and your partner are starting to notice flaws and characteristics that might get in the way of the "ideal". The fact is, there is no ideal. There is no perfection except a perfect imperfection – that means that you and your partner should be able to accept each other with flaws and traits, likewise, in case you truly love each other. As mentioned earlier in the book, acceptance, recognition and appreciation are some of the key qualities of a happy and healthy relationship. Don't be afraid to dig deeper, and don't be afraid to open yourself to your partner. One of relationship-strengthening activities that may help you improve your relationship at the very start, is getting to know each other better through a series of exercises for couples. For starters, you can exchange your favorite books, play favorite music to each other and agree to watch each other's favorite movies together. You may also get involved in quiz talk, asking your partner "trivia" questions that you believe would reveal a bit more about your partner's characteristics. For example, if you are watching a horror movie, you may ask your partner what is his biggest fear. Every shared activity with your partner is another way of getting closer to knowing each other better. By sharing your favorite books, music, movies and other personal things that your partner may be interested in, you are actually sharing a piece of your own characteristics and preferences, that way deepening intimacy and connection. Moreover, you are getting a hold of appreciation for differences and similarities that describe you as a couple.

No Dwelling Allowed

Couples fight, argue, can encounter disagreements, and tend to enter conflicts out of numerous different reasons – and as we emphasized on more than several occasions through the book, this is a perfectly normal thing in any relationship, including romantic relationships (perhaps, especially romantic relationships). Conflicts and disagreements arise as a way of testing the strength of a relationship, while failing often means not putting enough effort in resolving problems you might have with your partner. Conflicts may "pack up" to create more serious issues and may result in losing intimacy and connection you have with your partner, which furthermore may shake the very foundation of your relationship. Before you allow this to happen, you and your partner can work on preventive measures through couples' activities for strengthening. Whenever you and your partner enter a conflict or encounter a disagreement, make sure that you are able to resolve this conflict and find an agreement before the end of the day and before you hit the bed. In case conflicts are left unresolved, you are tempted to dwell on the argument you are having with your partner, coming up with worst-case scenarios in your head and widening the gap between you and your partner. Instead of working on resolving the problem, some couples allow anger and dwelling to kick in, making the problem even worse and unattended, which furthermore may create issues in communication as well. To avoid making your conflicts worse, try to resolve your arguments within the same day you entered a conflict with your partner. Clear communication – talking and listening on turns, while using logic and truth – is the best way of successfully resolving disagreements. If you are not able to resolve a conflict with the same day the conflict started, you may agree to give the argument a rest for a couple of days until you are able to figure out whether the fight you are having is worth fighting in the first place.

Stressors: Identification and Elimination
We already talked about the effects that external factors and outside stressors can

leave on a couple, along the way affecting the harmony and dynamics of your relationship. Stressors may test your relationship to the furthest points where it may even jeopardize it – however, there is something you and your partner can do to prevent that and make your relationship stronger. This activity will help you connect with your partner, while learning how to appreciate each other's sensitivity and vulnerability to stressors. Moreover, this exercise should help you practice mutual support with your partner. Make sure that you are able to identify stressors and work on eliminating and diminishing external factors that are negatively affecting you, your partner, and your relationship. Stress factors should be identified and eliminated primarily because factors such as depression, illness, problems with finances or problems at work, can seriously damage your relationship. This is the case because we are sometimes stressed with numerous factors to the point where we are ready to vent our anger, insecurities, fear and other negative emotions, regardless of whether it is affecting the relationship with our partner. In case you are constantly stressed out, the chances are that you will release some of this tension on the cost of your partner's peace, which will push you into a conflict. Try to eliminate and identify stressors together with your partner to avoid negative case scenarios. It is perfectly fine to argue when there is a problem between you that needs to be resolved – however, venting due to the effects of stressors may only create a series of conflicts that are difficult to resolve until the real source of the problem is found and eliminated. So, for instance, if you are depressed, you need to talk to your partner about it to raise awareness on the fact that something is not quite right. Moreover, you may find an ally in your partner in eliminating and identifying the source of your depression. You may also choose to talk to a therapist towards finding a solution. In case you have problems at work, instead of relieving your stress in a way that would affect your partner and your relationship, you may talk to your partner and ask for advice, while letting your partner know that you have a problem that causing you stress. Any problem can be resolved when identified, while getting recognition, acceptance and understanding from your partner will make your relationship stronger.

No Excuse for a "Busy" Life

So, you and your partner are committed to numerous obligations and might be in need of superb multitasking skills in order to take care of everything you need to do in a day. As a consequence, you have little room for spending some alone time with your partner. This type of case scenario can result in losing a connection you have with your partner, while emphasizing the lack of attention, appreciation and intimacy. If you are too busy and always too tired to spend some alone time with your partner, you may unintentionally convince your partner that you don't care enough to commit. Regardless of how busy and hectic your everyday schedule may be, you NEED to find some time for your partner in case you are motivated to keep your relationship alive and functioning. You can agree to spend more time together, while setting up the mandatory day off from all other commitments in order to dedicate yourself to each other. Make sure to schedule at least one mandatory date a week – the more, the better.

Cuddling

Cuddling, smooching, kissing, holding hands – physical intimacy needs to be practiced through touch and physical connection. Forget about stress, obligations and everything else that may act as a stressor or distraction, and enjoy your partner's company. Relationships grow stronger with enhanced intimacy as romantic relationship simply need physical connection – and that is a pure fact. The lack of physical intimacy may make your partner believe that she/he is neglected, doesn't matter to you, while it may also convince your partner that you are losing interest in your relationship. This is a rather simple and rewarding activity for couples and it asks only for free time and free will. Lie or sit beside your partner, hug each other, kiss, hold hands, cuddle – be physically intimate and enjoy these moments of bliss as you are working on strengthening your relationship.

Keeping it Fresh

Keeping your relationship interesting and dynamic doesn't need to be that hard even though it may sometimes appear that you need to put an extra effort to make things work with your partner. Aside from spending time together, finding mutual hobbies and interests, and practicing intimacy, there is another strengthening activity for couples that may help you keep your relationship dynamics fresh. You and your partner can agree on trying or doing something new together every week (or every month if you feel like weekly basis is too much to handle). For example, you may decide to go to that new Lebanese restaurant that just opened in your town and try their cuisine, or there is a new club opening next week. Never done a bungee jump together (or individually)? Why not try it together? Did you find an interesting position you can use in bed and that you believe your partner would appreciate? Take action! Each partner needs to come up with a new activity that would represent the first-time activity for both partners. Having "first times" together will make your relationship stronger while deepening your connection and making your relationship fresh, interesting and dynamic.

Sharing is Caring

When we refer to a handily rhymed phrase "sharing is caring" we don't necessarily address the physical part of sharing where you and your partner may have a shared bank account, are sharing room, home, bills, and so on. We are rather addressing the more abstract part of sharing – sharing your thoughts, opinion, fears and doubts, plans, goals and other important things that define you as a person. You and your partner may create an additional support for your relationship by sharing the way you feel, perceive and plan your future. That way, you will be able to know each other better, while sharing a connection along the way. You can practice sharing on everyday basis – for example, if you are having your morning coffee together, both partners can share their plans for the day. What is most important in that plan is not to leave out some time for your partner – even if you have only an hour to spare before you go to bed. By sharing your thoughts, opinions, believes, goals and plans, you are actually strengthening the bond between you and your partner, also letting your partner know that you value their own thoughts, opinions, plans, goals and beliefs. Additionally, by sharing your personal thoughts and plans, you are letting your partner know that you trust them.

Alone Time Matters

As we already made it clear in one of the previous sections in the guide, spending more time together is crucial for perseverance of your relationship, however, having some "me" time also matters. Alone time in strengthening activities for couples? Even though it may appear as odd, this is exactly what both partners need in order to be able to function together. Regardless of how much you love spending time with your partner and regardless of how great it feels when you are together as a couple, both partners would still use some healthy "me" time. In case you are sharing a living space, this activity comes as even more important as it may represent a great way of practicing your individual growth. As well as you are making a commitment to work on your relationship, you should likewise dedicate to your own personal goals and self-improvement. That way, you will be able to give more to your relationship as you are growing as a person and progressing in completing your personal goals. You can have physical and mental "alone time". In the first case, you may isolate yourself for a day or for several hours, as you wish, and dedicate to an activity that matters to you on a personal and individual level. Whether you are working on a project, planting a garden or just relaxing with some of your favorite music, you need to take advantage of your alone time the best way possible. Some people need alone time more often as this is a way they are able to "charge batteries", so don't be confused or offended in case your partner has a greater need to spend some time alone when compared to your need for "me" time. You can freely discuss any doubts or fears that you might have regarding this case. Just be open, honest, and have some trust in your partner.

Now that we have listed some of the top relationship-strengthening activities for couples who are looking for ways to prevent their relationship from going downhill, we are moving onto the next chapter where you will find worksheets and techniques for couples that should help you and your partner with maintaining a healthy and happy relationship.

Chapter 9: How To Recognize Toxic And Unhealthy Behavior?

Anxiety isn't always the element that affects a relationship. Sometimes it's the other path around, and the reason you have anxiety is because of a toxic relationship. But what exactly does toxic mean? We refer to a toxic relationship when it isn't beneficial to you, and it's harmful somehow. The building blocks for a healthy relationship are made from mutual respect and admiration, but sometimes it just isn't enough.

However, there is a difference between a problematic relationship and a toxic one, mainly the noxious atmosphere surrounding you. This kind of relationship can suffocate you with time and prevent you from living a happy, productive life. Many factors lead to toxicity. It is most often caused by friction between two people who are opposites of each other. In others, nothing specific is to blame, and the toxic relationship grows from the lack of communication, the establishment of boundaries, and the ability to agree on something, or at the very least, compromise.

Take note that not all toxic relationships develop because of the couple. Sometimes there is an outlier seeking to influence conflict because they will benefit from it in some way. This type of individual preys on other people's insecurities, weaknesses, or manipulates his way inside a relationship from which he has something to gain. In some cases, a toxic person seeks to destroy a relationship to get closer to one of them. Personal needs, emotions, and goals take priority over anyone else's well-being.

With that in Mind, Let's Briefly Explore the Characteristics of a Toxic Relationship:

Poisonous: A relationship that is extremely unpleasant to be around as it poisons the atmosphere around it. It makes anyone around the couple anxious, and it can even lead to psychological and emotional problems such as anxiety and depression.

Deadly: Toxic relationships are bad for your health. In many cases, it involved risky, destructive, and abusive behaviors. Some people end up harming themselves with alcohol, drugs, or worse. Injuries and even death can become the final result.

Negative: In this kind of relationship, negativity is the norm. There is no positive reinforcement, even when children are involved. The overwhelming lack of approval and emotional support is standard.

Harmful: Toxic relationships, lack balance, and awareness. Those involved are never truly aware of each other and lack the most positive principles that a healthy relationship needs. Toxicity also promotes immoral and malicious acts that harm a romantic relationship.

As mentioned earlier, toxic relationships don't always involve psychopaths or those who display similar traits. In many situations, these relationships are the way they are due to decent people who are terrible decision-makers or lack social skills. Taking a wrong turn in life happens to everyone, and many people change, but not always for the better.

Warning Signs

Now that you can better identify toxic relationships and the kind of involved people, let's see if you're in one or not. Humans are complex creatures, and the traits don't necessarily make someone toxic. Some underlying issues and disorders can make people behave negatively. However, they can still be excellent partners. With that said, here's a list of questions you can ask yourself to learn more about your relationship:

How do you feel in the company of your partner?

Do you feel happy, safe, and nurtured in the presence of your significant other?

Are all the other people involved in your relationship safe and happy? For instance, your children (if you have any), parents, friends, and so on. As mentioned earlier, people tend to avoid toxic relationships instead of being in contact with them.

Do you experience anxiety or panic attacks when discussing something with your partner?

Can you think of any scenarios in which you were manipulated to do something that wasn't for your best interest?

Is your partner pushing the limits of what you would consider ethical? Is he or she even crossing the line of what is legal?

Does your partner to push you to perform challenging tasks that you consider entirely unnecessary? These challenges may seem pointless, and that you need to resolve just because it's what your partner wants.

Do you feel emotionally strained and exhausted after interacting with your partner?

Handling a toxic Relationship

As mentioned, a toxic relationship can be a powerful source of anxiety. It doesn't have to be a romantic relationship either. Some of them you can avoid by cutting contact with some people to feel relief. However, there are certain people you simply cannot break away from, whether they are romantic partners or your mother in law.

The first step is to accept the inescapable situation. When your options are limited, you cannot achieve relief by avoidance, and acceptance leads to a decrease in anxiety. You may be tempted to be hostile towards that person, but it won't help. Instead, it will just add to your worries and stress. At this point, your only alternative is managing your anxiety by admitting to yourself that you may never be able to get along with that person. Besides, you can attempt to ignore him or her entirely by never spending time together and ignoring any contact. However, none of these tactics usually work.

Accept that this relationship is complicated and challenges you, but you do your best to make it better. That doesn't mean you should completely surrender. Accepting your situation will allow yourself new possibilities and new options instead of repeatedly punishing yourself.

Take note that you need to be consciously aware that you are not responsible for anyone else's emotions and reactions for the process of acceptance to take hold. Toxic behavior often makes people blame you for their situation and feelings. Do not accept any of that, as you are not the reason for their suffering. They need to take responsibility for their thoughts and actions instead of blaming others.

The second step is telling the truth. If a toxic relationship is creating stress, you often lie to avoid conflict, causing even more anxiety. The problem is that when you lie to such a person, you enable them and become partially responsible for the reality they create — leading to the toxic environment surrounding them.

Chapter 10: Relationship And The Role Of Mutual Blame

These are just a few examples of how people in relationships blame one another. I am sure the reader can come up with many more from their relationships. What is important to understand about mutual blame is that it never works. It is usually in the context of arguments that a couple starts to engage in the process of mutual blame. Once that happens the couple starts to become defensive and angrier than at the start. Being told you are to blame for something is being told you are incompetent, at fault, and lacking in many ways. No one wants to feel backed into a corner and forced to confess to being wrong. Because one's pride and ego become involved, it becomes necessary to prove the other person wrong and to then blame then. Even knowing that they are to blame for something, a partner will deny they are responsible. In the case above, he probably was asked to buy a container of milk. However, because they were in the midst of an argument he probably denied that he forgot and blamed her.

The nature of relationships is such that everyone is at fault because everyone contributes, in some way, to the problem. In other words, people in a relationship impact one another in dozens of ways. The fact that they impact one another provides a good and convenient reason to engage in blame. In reality, rarely, anyone is totally to blame for many of the things that happen. Relating means that interactions are going on between two people who have a history and future together. Interaction does not mean that one partner caused something to happen to the other. Each individual is responsible for their behaviors, separate and apart from the other. For example, if I had a bad day, it does not mean that my partner caused it. Another example might be that "I withdraw from interacting because of your criticisms" really means that "I feel like I want to withdraw when I hear criticism." An age-old example is that "you gave me a headache." In reality, I have a headache." Why blame it on another person?

In the end, it is better, when in a conflict, to find ways to find solutions to the disagreement. Sometimes it is as simple as finding a better way to phrase things. Communication is more than one individual speaking. Rather, communication means listening first and then responding in non-defensive ways. For example, using the pronoun "I" when speaking is far better than accusatory "you." Also, the use of the word "why" as in "why do you" is accusatory. It sounds a lot better to say "I am so angry that I got laid off that I want to blame everyone." Another example is to say "I wish we could find a solution that you would find acceptable. The choice of words is always important. In a permanent relationship, the goal should not be to win an argument at the expense of the other person, not if you value that person. In close relations, winning an argument can mean losing the relationship.

Rather Than Blame, Find Solutions.

Toxic Relationships: What They Are And 8 Types Of Toxic Individuals

With few exceptions, human beings want to be emotionally and physically close to each other. Life seems better shared. And yet no area of human endeavor seems more fraught with challenges and difficulties than our relationships with others. Relationships, like most things in life worth having, require effort.

Think Of It This Way: Even good relationships take work. After all, our significant other, our close friends, and even our parents aren't perfect (and, oddly enough, they may not see us as perfect either). We have to learn how to accommodate and adapt to their idiosyncrasies, their faults, their moods, etc., just as they must learn how to do the same with us. And it's worth it.

Some relationships, however, are more difficult and require proportionately more work. We are not clones but individuals, and some individuals in relationships are going to have more difficulties, more disagreements. But because we value these relationships we're willing to make the effort it takes to keep them.

And then there are toxic relationships. These relationships have mutated themselves into something that has the potential, if not corrected, to be extremely harmful to our well being. These relationships are not necessarily hopeless, but they require substantial and difficult work if they are to be changed into something healthy. The paradox is that to have a reasonable chance to turn a toxic relationship into a healthy relationship, we have to be prepared to leave it (more about this later).

So What Exactly Is A Toxic Relationship And How Do You Know If You're In One?

By definition, a toxic relationship is a relationship characterized by behaviors on the part of the toxic partner that are emotionally and, not infrequently, physically damaging to their partner. While a healthy relationship contributes to our self-esteem and emotional energy, a toxic relationship damages self-esteem and drains energy. A healthy relationship involves mutual caring, respect, and compassion, an interest in our partner's welfare and growth, and the ability to share control and decision-making, in short, a shared desire for each other's happiness. A healthy relationship is a safe relationship, a relationship where we can be ourselves without fear, a place where we feel comfortable and secure. A toxic relationship, on the other hand, is not a safe place. A toxic relationship is characterized by insecurity, self-centeredness, dominance, control. We risk our very being by staying in such a relationship. To say a toxic relationship is dysfunctional is, at best, an understatement.

Keep in mind that it takes two individuals to have a toxic relationship. Initially, we'll look at the behaviors of the toxic partner, but we must look equally hard at the individual who is the recipient of the toxic behavior. And we must ask, Why? Why does an adult stay in a relationship that will almost inevitably damage him or her emotionally and/or physically? And what, if anything can we do short of leaving that might help mend such a relationship? We'll examine both these questions later. First, however, let's examine toxic behaviors and relationships in more detail.

Types Of Toxic Relationships

Even a good relationship may have brief periods of behaviors we could label toxic on the part of one or both partners. Human beings, after all, are not perfect. Few of us have had any formal education on how to relate to others. We often have to learn as we go, hoping that our basic style of relating to significant others often learned from our parents and/or friends is at least reasonably effective. As mentioned above, however, dysfunction is the norm in a toxic relationship. The toxic partner engages in inappropriate controlling and manipulative behaviors on pretty much a daily basis. Paradoxically, to the outside world, the toxic partner often behaves in an exemplary manner.

Note: Any relationship involving physical violence or substance abuse is by definition extremely toxic and requires immediate intervention and, with very few exceptions, separation of the two partners. While these relationships are not necessarily irreparable, I cannot emphasize too much how destructive they are. If you're in such a relationship, get help now!

A toxic individual behaves the way he or she does essentially for one main reason: he or she must be in complete control and must have all the power in his or her relationship. Power-sharing does not occur in any significant way in a toxic relationship. And while power struggles are normal in any relationship, particularly in the early stages of a marriage, toxic relationships are characterized by one partner insisting on being in control. Keep in mind, the methods used by such an individual to control his or her partner in a toxic relationship may or may not be readily apparent, even to their partner.

With the above in mind, let's examine some of the more common types of dysfunctional behaviors that a toxic partner may use in a relationship with a significant other. These categories should not be seen as exclusive. Frequently, a toxic individual will use several types of controlling behaviors to achieve his or her ends. Also, while the examples below are most typically seen in marriages and /or other committed relationships, they can certainly occur in parent-child interactions or friendships.

A Further Note: For the sake of brevity, I'll often use the word "victim" to refer to the recipient of toxic behavior. In reality, however, this individual is not a victim, at least not in the sense that they are helpless to do anything about their relationship.

1. Deprecator-Belittler

This type of toxic individual will constantly belittle you. He or she will make fun of you, essentially implying that pretty much anything you say that expresses your ideas, beliefs, or wants is silly or stupid. A toxic partner will not hesitate to belittle you in public, in front of your friends or family. Even though you may have asked your toxic partner to stop belittling you, he or she will continue this behavior, occasionally disguising it by saying, "I'm just kidding. Can't you take a joke?" The problem is they are not kidding and what they're doing is not a joke. The toxic partner wants all the decision making power. Unfortunately, if you tolerate this deprecating behavior long enough, you very well may begin to believe you can't make good decisions.

This type of toxic individual will often tell you that you're lucky to have them as a partner, that no other man or woman would want you. His or her goal is to keep your self-esteem as low as possible so that you don't challenge their absolute control of the relationship.

2. The "Bad Temper" Toxic Partner

Frequently I'll have a client who will tell me they've given up trying to argue or disagree with their partner because he/she gets so angry or loses his or her temper, and then often won't interact with them in any meaningful way for days. "Controlling by intimidation" is the classic behavior of a toxic partner.

Often these individuals have an unpredictable and "hair-trigger" temper. Their partners often describe themselves as "walking on eggshells" around the toxic partner, never quite knowing what will send him or her into a rage. This constant need for vigilance and inability to know what will trigger an angry outburst wears on both the "victim's" emotional and physical health.

Again, it is noteworthy that this type of emotionally abusive partner rarely shows this side of his or her self to the outside world. He or she is frequently seen as a pleasant, easy-going person who almost everyone likes. As you would expect, if you confront a "bad temper" partner about the inappropriateness of their anger, they will almost always blame their temper outburst on you. Somehow it's your fault they yell and scream. This disowning of responsibility for their dysfunctional behavior is typical of a toxic partner.

3. The Guilt-Inducer

A toxic relationship can, of course, occur not only between two individuals in a committed relationship but also between friends or parents and their adult children. Control in these relationships, as well as in a committed relationship, is exercised by inducing guilt in the "victim." The guilt inducer controls by encouraging you to feel guilty any time you do something he or she doesn't like. Not infrequently they will get someone else to convey their sense of "disappointment" or "hurt" to you. For example, your father calls up to tell you how disappointed your mother was that you didn't come over for Sunday dinner. A guilt inducer not only controls by inducing guilt but also by temporarily "removing" guilt if you end up doing what he or she wants you to do. For guilt-prone individuals, anything or anyone that removes guilt is very desirable and potentially almost addictive, so the guilt inducer has an extremely powerful means of control at their disposal.

Incidentally, guilt induction is the most common form of control used by a toxic parent(s) to control their adult children. Frequently, a spouse or significant other will disguise their guilt-inducing control by seemingly supporting a decision you make – i.e., going back to school – but will then induce guilt by subtly reminding you of how much the children miss you when you're gone, or how you haven't been paying much attention to him or her lately, etc. As with all toxic behaviors, guilt-inducing is designed to control your behavior so your toxic partner, parent, or a friend gets what he or she wants.

4. The Overreactor/Deflector

If you've ever tried to tell a significant other that you're unhappy, hurt, or angry about something they did and somehow find yourself taking care of their unhappiness, hurt, or anger, you're dealing with an overreactor/deflector. You find yourself comforting them instead of getting comfort yourself. And, even worse, you feel bad about yourself for being "so selfish" that you brought up something that "upset" your partner so much. Needless to say, your initial concern, hurt, or irritation gets lost as you remorsefully take care of your partner's feelings.

A variation on this theme is the deflector: You try and express your anger or irritation regarding some issue or event your spouse stays out with his/her friends two hours longer than they said they would and doesn't even bother to call and somehow your toxic partner finds a way to make this your fault!

5. The Over-Dependent Partner

Odd as it may seem, one method of toxic control is for your partner to be so passive that you have to make most decisions for them. These toxic controllers want you to make virtually every decision for them, from where to go to dinner to what car to buy. Remember, not deciding is a decision that has the advantage of making someone else – namely you – responsible for the outcome of that decision. And, of course, you'll know when you've made the "wrong" decision by your partner's passive-aggressive behavior such as pouting or not talking to you because you chose a movie or restaurant they didn't enjoy. Or you choose to go to spend the weekend with your parents and your partner goes along but doesn't speak to anyone for two days.

Passivity can be an extremely powerful means of control. If you're involved in a relationship with a passive controller, you'll likely experience constant anxiety and/or fatigue, as you worry about the effect of your decisions on your partner and are drained by having to make virtually every decision.

6. The "Independent" (Non-Dependable) Toxic Controller

This individual frequently disguises his or her toxic controlling behavior as simply asserting his or her "independence." "I'm not going to let anyone control me" is their motto. This toxic individual will only rarely keep his or her commitments. What these individuals are up to is controlling you by keeping you uncertain about what they're going to do. Non-dependables will say they'll call you, they'll take the kids to a movie Saturday, they'll, etc. etc., but then they don't. Something always comes up. They usually have a plausible excuse, but they simply don't keep their commitments. As a result, they control you by making it next to impossible for you to make commitments or plans.

What's even more distressing is that this type of toxic individual does not make you feel safe and secure in your relationship. It's not just their behavior that's unpredictable; you're never quite sure that they are emotionally committed to you, that you and your relationship with them are a priority in their life. You'll often find yourself asking for reassurance from them, reassurance that they love you, find you attractive, are committed to your marriage, etc. Their response is often just vague enough to keep you constantly guessing, and is designed to keep you doing what they want to "earn" their commitment. The anxiety you feel in such a relationship can, and often do, eat away at your emotional and physical health.

7. The User

Users especially at the beginning of a relationship often seem to be very nice, courteous, and pleasant individuals. And they are, as long as they're getting everything they want from you. What makes a relationship with a user toxic is its one-way nature and the fact that you will end up never having done enough for them. Users are big-time energy drainers who will leave you if they find someone else who will do more for them.

An adept user will occasionally do some small thing for you, usually something that doesn't inconvenience or cost them too much. Be warned: they have not given you a gift, they've given you an obligation. If you ever balk at doing something for them or doing things their way, they'll immediately hold whatever they've done over your head and work hard to induce guilt.

8. The Possessive (Paranoid) Toxic Controller

This type of toxic individual is really bad news. Early in your relationship with them, you may appreciate their "jealousy," particularly if it isn't too controlling. And most, but certainly not all, possessives will imply that once the two of you are married or in a committed relationship, they'll be just fine.

These toxic individuals will become more and more suspicious and controlling as time goes on. They'll check the odometer in your car to make sure you haven't gone somewhere you "shouldn't," they'll interrogate you if you have to stay late at work, they will, in short, make your life miserable. Over time they will work hard to eliminate any meaningful relationships you have with friends, and sometimes even with family. They do not see themselves in a relationship with you; they see themselves as possessing you. Your efforts to reassure a toxic possessive about your fidelity and commitment to them will be in vain. If you stay in a relationship with such an individual you will cease to have a life of your own.

Further Thoughts

Angry millennial couple arguing shouting blaming each other of problem, frustrated husband and annoyed wife quarreling about bad marriage relationships, unhappy young family fighting at home concept

Keep in mind that the toxicity of the above individuals is a matter of degree. You may have experienced some, if not all, of these behaviors — hopefully in a mild form — occasionally in your relationships. And that's the keyword: occasionally. In a toxic relationship, these behaviors are the norm, not the exception. Most of us manipulate once in a while, play helpless, induce guilt, etc. We're not perfect nor are our relationships. What distinguishes a toxic relationship is both the severity of these behaviors and how frequently they occur. So why do people behave in toxic ways and why do others put up with such behaviors? The answer is the same for both individuals:

Poor self-esteem rooted in underlying insecurity. Toxic individuals behave the

way they do because, at some level, they
don't believe they are lovable and/or that
anyone would willingly want to meet their
needs. Their partners stay with toxic
individuals because they too believe they
are unlovable and that no one would
willingly meet their needs.

But aren't controlling individuals often
narcissistic, don't they simply have inflated
egos, believe they're entitled to everything
they want at no cost to themselves?

Occasionally, particularly in the case of the
toxic user, narcissism may be part of the
problem, but narcissism itself is often a
reaction to underlying insecurity.

This brings up the question and the
problem of what to do if you're in a toxic
relationship. Many of my clients initially
come to me with the hope that I will give
them a magical tool that will "fix" their
toxic partner, or, at the very least, for me
to sympathize with them and agree on
how bad their partner is. While catharsis
may give temporary relief, it isn't lasting.
And while there certainly are things an
individual can do to attempt to change the

way a toxic partner behaves, most of my clients are often hesitant to do them, fearing their toxic partner may leave the relationship.

The Paradox Is This: If you want to improve your relationship with a toxic partner, you have to be willing to leave that relationship if nothing changes. If you're unwilling to do so, you have very limited power available to you. Your toxic partner will know ultimately, regardless of what they do, you really won't leave.

So before you attempt to confront a toxic partner, make sure your self-esteem and self-confidence are good enough for you to know that you will be all right if they end the relationship with you (or you end up having to end it with them). If you're not there I strongly urge you to get therapeutic help and/or to join a co-dependency group.

What To Do

The bad news is that you cannot change your partner. The good news is that you can change yourself which may lead you to behave differently with your partner, resulting in your partner deciding to change his or her behavior. Essentially what you do is calmly but firmly confront the toxic behavior. You do this by identifying the behavior(s) to your partner, letting him or her know they are no longer acceptable, and suggesting alternate behaviors that would work better. Simple, isn't it?

It is once again, you have to believe you deserve to be treated with courtesy, compassion, and respect in a relationship or you will not continue the relationship. When you first confront a toxic partner you can expect that he or she will escalate their controlling behaviors. You have to be able to handle whatever they do. You have to stay calm and firm and simply repeat your request. If your partner refuses to change, consider separating from the relationship for 30 days. You should then talk with them again, repeat your requests, and let them know that you will not stay in the relationship if they continue their toxic behavior. If they once again refuse to change, you need to end the relationship. If they promise to change but relapse, repeat the cycle one more time. The bottom line: you can attempt to seriously improve a toxic relationship only if you're prepared to leave it.

A Notable Exception: I believe strongly in a "zero tolerance" policy for physical abuse. No matter how apologetic your partner is, if you've been physically abused you must separate from them immediately. If they then seek appropriate help and you have reasonable confidence that they will not physically abuse you again, you may consider whether or not you want to return to the relationship.

What if you have a parent(s) who behave in a toxic manner? Fortunately, as an adult child, you do not live with them 24/7, and you likely have the support of a significant other in dealing with them. Essentially you need to deal with a toxic parent in the same way you would deal with a toxic partner: You confront the controlling behavior, offer alternative ways the two (or three) of you could relate, and see what happens. If your parent(s) refuse to change their behavior which, as mentioned above, will usually be controlled by toxic guilt induction, you will need to severely limit their contact with you. Since few of us would, or should, totally abandon an elderly parent who may need our help, you'll probably maintain some contact with them, but you'll need to take control of the relationship. Not an easy task, but by taking control – for example by limiting phone calls, or by you choosing when you do or do not see them, etc. – you may be able to offer them the help they need while keeping your emotional equilibrium.

Stop Playing The Blame Game: Take Responsibility In Your Relationship

Taking ownership and responsibility for your actions is an important part of healthy relationships. Doing so is an empowering reminder that you have control over the role you play in your relationship. Taking responsibility creates trust and dependability. When you take responsibility for your behaviors, you demonstrate to your partner your willingness, to be honest, and vulnerable, which in turn encourages your partner to be open and authentic with you.

Being in the throes of my first relationship ever, I have learned a lot about myself. By being willing to accept that everyone makes mistakes, we learn how to take responsibility and grow. I have realized that some of my behavior was unhealthy, and I chose to take responsibility for it. Recently, codependency was something my partner and I talked through. I recognized that I was relying too much on their affection and support and was not as engaged with supporting them. The support dynamic was imbalanced, and it showed in my low levels of self-confidence and need for my partner to be my only source of self-worth. When we communicated and I recognized that changing my behavior could make our relationship better, I took responsibility for working to change how we supported each other in the relationship. I was able to recognize the mutual importance of support, and this helped me grow in my relationship.

What Taking Responsibility Looks Like

It is important to distinguish between taking and deflecting responsibility for both you and your partner. Be aware of defensive responses which might include "stop being so sensitive" or "I didn't know that you cared about that" or "you should've said something." It's not only important for you to take responsibility. Your partner must learn and do as well to have a healthy relationship. For you, taking responsibility looks like practicing self-awareness. Another way is being able to apologize and accept that what you do affects your partner. For your partner, taking responsibility looks like having open communication with you about their feelings and being willing to admit they can grow from the hard parts of the relationship. Your partner learns to take responsibility when they own their behaviors and hold themselves accountable for their actions.

Accepting Misplaced Blame

There is an extremely important difference between taking responsibility and accepting misplaced blame. Taking responsibility is never accepting blame for things you didn't do. For example, when your partner tells you that something is your fault, you don't automatically take responsibility for whatever mistake it was. It's common in unhealthy relationships, particularly codependent ones, for one person (the manipulator) to say, "it's all your fault" and for his/her partner to say "it's all my fault." A lot of times, people may take responsibility for things that are not their fault, and they might even do so without consciously realizing it. Making excuses for your partner's behavior or yourself is unhealthy and may lead to these unhealthy behaviors being ignored or accepted.

How To Practice This In Real Life

Taking responsibility is not just a one-sided practice. The following ways to use the empowering action of taking responsibility is important for both you and your partner to use and practice in your relationship.

1. Be Honest

"You have to love yourself before you love others" is a versatile phrase that has multiple meanings when applied to relationships. It can translate to "You have to be honest with yourself before you can be honest with others." Being honest with yourself begins with a healthy sense of self-awareness. And being self-aware means you acknowledge that what you say and do impacts your partner.

For Example: Referring back to the mustard situation, imagine you're Jill. A healthy response would be to take ownership of her actions and respond with something like, "Oh, I'm sorry! I should have asked you before I added mustard. I did not realize you didn't like mustard, and this is my mistake."

2. Act On Situations, Don't React

When people are held accountable for their behaviors, they often become defensive. Getting defensive is a reaction. When you act on a situation, you can respond with clarity and awareness. You can practice acting on situations instead of

163

reacting by taking deep breaths or counting to ten. It also helps to take a second and look at the situation from your partner's perspective. It can be hard to think from the other perspective, especially in the heat of the moment. By being honest with yourself and your partner, you can effectively respond by taking responsibility.

For Example: Jill is reacting to Jack being upset instead of acting on her need to take responsibility. Acting instead of reacting allows you to clearly define a self-aware and honest answer to unhealthy behavior.

3. Be Willing To Forgive Your Partner And Yourself

Everyone makes mistakes and forgiving yourself or your partner is important for moving past challenges and making your relationship stronger. When you view taking responsibility for your mistakes as an opportunity to learn, your relationship can become a place that fosters and celebrates growth. Forgiveness builds trust and accountability in your relationship, breaks down resentment, and stops the never fun "blame game."

Taking responsibility for your behaviors in your relationship requires honest and open communication and a willingness to address unhealthy excuses with your partner. They're not always easy discussions to have, but you'll find that doing so builds trust within your relationship over time and is an empowering way to learn and grow.

Chapter 11: Managing Crisis Situations

As we have seen in previous chapters, sooner or later, for any couple there will be the period of crisis.

The important thing is to know how to face it in the right way.

If you are reading this guide and if you want to put its contents into practice, you will surely face the moments of crisis based on a solid relationship focused on love and harmony.

However, in the pathological phase of the relationship, there are some elements that you need to focus on more, which can help you overcome the various difficulties and fights.

First, you need to understand the partner's reasons before acting or reacting to a certain behavior. You should not limit yourself to appearances before judging, but you should be willing to know the background, the way your partner was raised, the environment in which his or her personality developed.

We all carry within us the traumas and wounds of the past, some more clearly, others less so. Knowing everyone's history helps you understand certain behaviors that you would not understand if you stopped at appearances. Being sensitive to your partner's past can avoid many arguments and improve the relationship.

Secondly, you need to manage time well. Time is the most important resource we have: we can sell it to someone (e.g. the employer), but we cannot buy it. When faced with important decisions to make, especially about the couple's life, we need to spend the right amount of time.

It is also necessary to devote the necessary time to the couple's relationship to cultivate and nurture it with love and devotion. Both the amount of time you devote and the quality are important.

Especially if you're going through a crisis, devote less to work and more to your relationship. Don't relate to your partner only when you are tired from work and can't wait to sleep.

Don't live life in a monotonous, predictable or conflictual way. Set yourself small positive goals every day in order to live a happy relationship: make small gifts, small surprises that your partner does not expect. And don't go to bed unless you are sure that you have given your partner at least a little bit of joy during the day. Make every day special: build your couple's love nest every day.

Always offer your support and emotional outreach: behave with the other person the way you would like them to behave with you; apply the golden rule in the relationship as well.

Also, do not oppress the other person with restrictions, jealousies, prohibitions. The couple is not a prison: everyone must feel free, have their own spaces of autonomy and cultivate their passions. This is the only way the partner will feel free to be authentic and spontaneous with you. Always remember: nobody forces you to sleep in the same bed. Your law must be that of love.

Moreover, in times of crisis, it is even more necessary to be willing to accept differences in character, without wanting to change the partner. Every issue must be resolved through compromise and dialogue: giving something to the other's reasons avoids many quarrels and misunderstandings.

Another golden rule is to listen with interest and curiosity to the other person, without taking a critical attitude and without judging. Some people don't even listen to their partner's words and are ready to contradict them right away. Sometimes silence is golden and the partner is not looking for advice, they just want to be listened to and understood to feel better.

Finally, another way to improve your damaged relationship is to limit your reactions to the current situation you are facing, without bringing up similar circumstances or even unresolved different situations that happened in the past.

Many couples tend to throw things at each other that no longer have anything to do with the current situation, with the only consequence that a small problem can take on disproportionate dimensions.

Coping with infidelity

Your partner cheated on you? Do you feel like the world's falling apart on you and you feel like a loser?

I know how it feels because I have been in this situation several times.

First, I want to tell you that this situation is common to millions of people: statistics say that almost 50% of couples will find themselves in a similar situation.

Secondly, you need to analyze the reasons that led to this: have you neglected your partner? Have you had disagreements about fundamental values in life or irreconcilable character incompatibilities? Is it only the partner's fault, who tends to cheat?

There can be many reasons behind infidelity.

What matters now, after reflecting on the reasons for infidelity, is how do you want to deal with adultery: do you want to forgive, or should you acknowledge that that person is not for you?

The final decision will be up to you alone, because only you know how much you love that person, what your family situations are, what you can tolerate and what you cannot.

If you are only engaged, for instance, you may decide with fewer constraints how to behave; if you are married with children, your decision will also affect other people's lives.

My opinion, in general, is that if a person has cheated on us, it is useless to continue: the magic and trust has broken and it is difficult, albeit not impossible, to start again.

However, I do not judge; as a fiancé I forgave several times, even though I was aware that the story was over.

When it comes to feelings, one should not judge. Sometimes the human mind is weak.

An incident that made me think was my barber who committed suicide after being left by his girlfriend. A few days earlier he had asked an acquaintance of mine: "What do you think about those who commit suicide after being left?" And my acquaintance answered lightly: "They're stupid."

Sometimes, during a relationship, a partner completely and naively relies on a person who is not worthy of them, putting everything aside; friends, personal interests, sometimes even family.

In these cases, the eventual breakup has a devastating effect on the psyche of the person who has been cheated.

Therefore, I do not judge those who want to forgive and the purpose of this guide is also to give suggestions on how to rebuild the relationship.

If you have strong character, if you understand that that person is not for you, if that person makes you deny your basic principles, it is better to break up.

If, for instance, you are a fervent Catholic and a partner had cheated on you on the grounds that you are too traditionalist and do not share the practice of couple swapping, being condescending to them could be even more devastating in the long term than the separation.

However, if you have the will and the strength to leave or accept the breakup of the relationship after the infidelity, it is a good thing: it means that you know you deserve more; that you can find better and that person was not for you.

If you love that person madly and hope to salvage the relationship, I am telling you that's possible too. Surely it is difficult, because it takes a long period of reconstruction of the relationship to renew the initial trust and feelings of love and tranquility.

I know some couples who are happy after overcoming marital infidelity. The commitment to rebuild trust can certainly lead to strengthen the couple and live a happy love relationship.

I remember a while ago I went to a faith meeting held by Claudia Koll. I was so impressed by her faith and dedication to others that I find it absurd that she has participated in erotic films in the past.

If I had not seen these films with my own eyes, I wouldn't have believed it. This is just one of many examples of how a person can also change for the better.

Back to us, though, how to rebuild the couple, or at least not to lose that person if you are not ready? Let us make some general assumptions that apply to all couples.

Never be jealous and possessive. Even if you are, practice smoothing out this flaw. Think about it: what does jealousy bring? Certainly, unnecessary fights, and fights have a long-term effect on feelings, as we have seen in previous chapters.

Those who feel oppressed by their partner will repress a desire for freedom that could lead to the breakup of the relationship or infidelity. So, paradoxically, if you are obsessively jealous you might get a different result from what you wanted, your partner might look for another person who is more joyful, less quarrelsome and who makes them feel freer in general. Jealousy is a feeling that is natural in us, yet stupid at the same time, because it certainly does not bring any benefit within the couple.

Therefore, it is important to practice not to show possessiveness or jealousy. On the contrary, you have to be attractive: have a thousand interests, not depend on your partner, feel confident, entertain your partner and discover new things together.

What to do if you suspect that a woman or a man is cheating on you?

Same rule applies as above: first, keep calm and do not let yourself be carried away by anger and jealousy. If you get carried away with negative feelings, you will lose points and the relationship will suffer. Think that your rival wants nothing more than to take you down, making you seem jealous, possessive, and nervous in general.

So, what to do? If you are not particularly committed to your partner, if you are willing to break your bond in case, they cheat on you, look into it: the cheater always makes even coarse missteps. Not everyone is willing to tolerate infidelity and it is right to break it off and then look for a more honest and sincere person.

But what if you love your partner and you do not want to lose them for any reason in the world?

Act as if nothing happened: do not investigate and do not try to catch your partner in the act. If you catch your partner in the act of cheating on you, you will suffer whilst the two lovers will be joined more in their guilt.

Unfortunately, there is the fascination of the forbidden: people like what is nasty and if what they like also causes suffering in a person, the pleasure is multiplied.

Therefore, do not try to track down your partner at the location of the prohibited meeting; do not check their mobile phone and do not argue out of jealousy.

If you argue with your partner because of another man or woman, you will only be entertaining them during their amorous encounter. I have often witnessed couples of lovers laughing at their jealous husband or wife because of several episodes. There are women or men who, when their jealous partner calls, even have sex with their lover, for a pure erotic game.

These things may sound absurd, but I assure you that they are real things and reality often exceeds imagination. The human soul is complex and interpreting it comprehensively is a chimera.

So, if you want to keep your relationship, ignore the rival completely. Even if they' re a mutual acquaintance, don't mention their name. If the cheating partner asks you for an opinion about that person, you speak well, saying that they are nice people. If you say that they are a smart, dangerous, mysterious person who is hiding something, you will only increase your rival's points.

Well, if you think about it, it's something normal. When a parent wants to give advice to their kid about their ideal partner, they usually get the opposite effect. Love is a partly irrational feeling and what is not ideal often attracts the most.

Therefore, tolerate the rival: if you use the right techniques, you will be the winner.

If you want to win against your rival, improve yourself and your relationship: become an interesting, fun, confident person. Be affectionate, but at the same time make it clear that without that person you would have a thousand other opportunities. Take the advice I gave you in previous chapters.

Remember, you are in a position of advantage over your partner. You have an established relationship that is growing day by day. The partner may be experiencing the moment of initial passion, but then everything will end and the first differences in character will begin. If your bond is strong, sooner or later your rival will succumb, and you will stay with the woman or man you love.

What do you do if your partner confesses to cheating on you and asks you for forgiveness?

As I wrote above, you must follow your heart. If you love that person, why not give them another chance? **Errare humanum**

est and it could happen to anyone. Of course, it is necessary to rebuild the relationship, the trust that has been broken, but nothing is impossible: I know couples who have overcome this situation and are closer together than ever.

If you decide to salvage the relationship, however, you must take care not to constantly throw their mistake in the other person's face. You must never ask the details of the infidelity: it is better not to know than to continue to suffer for the past. If you touch the old wounds, they will never heal.

If you live the present always looking to the past your relationship will wear out, you will sever the bond and suffer twice.

So, it is important to create a new beginning with the person you love. You have decided to forgive, and the past no longer exists; besides, you cannot change the past. So, let's leave our skeletons in the closet!

What to do instead if the partner confesses the infidelity, does not want to end the story with you, but feels undecided on what to do?

In this case there are two different situations to deal with. The first case is when your partner asks you for a period of reflection. In this circumstance it is obvious that the outcome of this period will be negative.

The reflection period is nothing more than an excuse to gain time and have two people at your feet. In this case, you are the first to break it off: play it early and follow all the strategies I will explain in the next chapter.

If, on the other hand, the person you love, after confessing the infidelity, tells you that they have had, and still have, a period of sentimental disbandment, but does not ask you for any pause for reflection, in that case, if you love that person so much, forgive and move on.

In this case, it is likely your partner will cheat on you again. Avoid intercepting encounters with your rival, do not show jealousy; allow your partner to date the other person as well. If you fight because of the other person, you will play into the other person's hands.

If you really love your partner, it is wiser to share them and play even. Love is a militia and, with the right techniques, as I explained above, you will win against any rival. It will then be up to you to decide if it is worth continuing with the person you love or not. But you must decide as the winner, at your own pace and according to your wishes.

Chapter 12: Considering Couples Therapy

When someone is struggling with their mental health, regardless of whether or not they have a diagnosed condition, therapy can be very helpful. The same goes for relationships, whether there is a major problem or not. A lot of people believe couples counseling is just for people on the verge of breakdown, but the reality is that just about every couple can benefit. Communication can be very tricky and there are ups and downs in every relationship. A good counselor can facilitate difficult conversations, provide insight into what couples are trying to say, or just help a couple with communication techniques. This chapter describes different scenarios where therapy can help, as well as guidelines on finding the best therapist for you and your partner.

Reasons to consider couples therapy

When should a couple consider therapy? There are lots of scenarios where a relationship can benefit from the advice and guidance of a third party, and they aren't all emotionally catastrophic. Here are seven:

You don't trust each other

Trust is the glue that keeps a relationship together. If it's broken, either through emotional or physical cheating, lying about money, or lies about anything, the relationship stalls and starts to break down. Either one person within the couple or both no longer feel safe and secure. A therapist can help heal the division, facilitate vulnerability, and offer guidance on what to do next.

You fight all the time

Some couples argue more than others, but if you realize you are fighting with your partner more than you usually do, it's a sign that something is wrong. It could be about anything small or big. The issue is that most of your communication becomes contentious and stressful. A counselor can help you figure out why arguing has become your go-to communication style and what to do about it.

You just don't communicate well

You don't have to be in conflict with your partner to benefit from therapy. Sometimes, you and your partner just don't "get" each other. Communication-wise, it feels like you are ships passing in the night. It's always a struggle to express your thoughts and feelings about things, and you frequently feel misunderstood or even ignored. On the other hand, you might feel disconnected from your partner and unable to get anything out of them, emotionally. Maybe both are present in your relationship. A therapist can help you safely break down walls, be more vulnerable, and learn to communicate more.

You're going through a huge life change

Change is always difficult on a relationship, even if it's good change. It can throw off your normal routines, emotional state, and even your identity. Changes in relationships can include moving house, getting a new job, losing a job, losing a loved one, having kids, and soon. It can be very hard to express your feelings (and even identify your feelings) to your partner, so therapy can be very beneficial. They can help you and your partner be vulnerable and honest with each other, understand each other more, and strengthen your bond.

Physical intimacy is a point of conflict

Everyone (and every couple) is different when it comes to physical intimacy. It can cause a lot of conflict, especially if one person in the relationship feels rejected, neglected, or pressured physically. It's a very sensitive and emotional topic, and frustrations can flare. A therapist can help keep things cool and collected, and provide a safe space for vulnerability and honesty.

One (or both) people in the relationship have mental health issues

Mental health issues like depression, anxiety, bipolar, and more have a big effect on a relationship. Navigating a relationship can be especially tricky if only one of the people has the diagnosis, and is having trouble communicating their needs to their partner. Maybe you have social anxiety and wish your partner would be more considerate about triggers, or your partner (who isn't mentally ill) is confused about what to do when you go through a depression episode. A therapist can help you two communicate and understand each other better.

Something just feels "off"

Therapy isn't just for couples who know exactly what they want to talk about. If something just feels "off" or wrong about your relationship, you should strongly consider therapy. A therapist can help you identify areas and triggers where the discomfort is strongest, and express your feelings and fears to your partner in a clear, honest way. It may turn out that you two just needed a third party to help clarify some things, or it may reveal deeper issues that you can focus on.

What couples therapy isn't

Couples therapy is not a magic solution to all of your problems as a couple or as an individual. Not every relationship can (or should) be saved, so don't go into couples therapy expecting to walk out with a perfect, shiny new relationship. Couples therapy should teach you better communication, but communicating better may reveal things that let you know the relationship shouldn't continue. This isn't easy to hear, but it's important to accept that going to couples therapy may not give you the happy ending you expect.

Couples therapy should also not be treated as something that only happens in the therapist's office. Don't plan on going once a week or once every two weeks, and not doing anything else. That won't actually improve communication between you and your partner. Like regular therapy, most of the work is actually done **outside** of that hour or so window. The therapist's job is to help identify areas of conflict, give advice on what to do, and facilitate dialogue, but it's up to you and your partner to actually put things into action.

Are there couples who **shouldn't** go to therapy?

Believe it or not, there are certain circumstances where a couple should not go to couples therapy. If both people in the couple aren't willing to do work on themselves, feel painful emotions, and be vulnerable with their partner, couples therapy will not work. Instead, the best way to improve the relationship is through individual therapy.

Most couples therapists also don't recommend therapy for abusive relationships. Abuse doesn't go away through better communication; it's a deeper issue. The abuser will usually not take responsibility for their own actions, and will try to manipulate the therapy to get the end goal **they** want. This is usually total control over their partner, who blames themselves for the abuse. Couples therapy can actually be dangerous for the abusee, since anything they say in the therapist's office might trigger their partner's anger once they've left. According to The National Domestic Violence Hotline, abuse isn't a "relationship" problem, so it isn't something that couples therapy will help.

How to find the right therapist

For couples therapy to be effective, you need the right therapist. How do you track one down? Here are some tips:

Make sure the therapist is qualified

The very first step when searching for a couples therapist is making sure they're educated and have the right qualifications. Look up counselors on websites like the National Registry of Marriage-Friendly Therapists, The Gottman Institute Referral Directory, and the American Association of Marriage and Family Therapists. If you just Google therapists in your area or hear about one through word-of-mouth, make sure they are licensed to practice therapy. Look for licenses like LMFT (licensed marriage and family therapist) and EFT (emotionally-focused couple's therapy).

There's nothing wrong with asking a therapist questions about their qualifications. Some good ones include, "How long have you been practicing couples therapy?" and "What kind of advanced training do you have?"

Find out their opinion on marriage and divorce

Before committing to a therapist, it's a good idea to find out if they lean one way or the other when it comes to divorce. Some therapists really care about keeping marriages together, while others are neutral. It isn't really ethical to suggest divorce for a couple if they haven't brought it up, but it isn't unheard of. By knowing what the therapist's bias is, you can decide if they are the right fit for your relationship goals or not. You can ask questions like:

• Do you believe all marriages can be saved?

• What's your view on divorce?

• What circumstances would make you believe divorce is the best option for a couple?

Trust your gut

You should feel comfortable with your therapist. You should also feel like they "get" you, even when you have trouble expressing your feelings and thoughts as clearly as you would like. Therapists are trained for a reason; they should be able to listen and - if what you said is confusing - help you clarify it for yourself and your partner. It can take 2-3 sessions to feel comfortable, but if you still aren't at ease, it may be time to try another therapist. Don't worry about offending them. They aren't interested in wasting your time or theirs with a counseling partnership that isn't working. How do you know if the therapist isn't the right fit? Watch out for signs and feelings like:

● They're always siding with your partner and you feel ganged up on.

● They're pressuring you to do something you don't want to do.

● You don't feel like the therapist is on the same page about your relationship goals.

● You don't feel respected or listened to.

● They think there's one "right" way of doing things and having a successful marriage.

- They're using language that makes you feel ashamed of your feelings and judged.

While you're deciding if a therapist is the right one for you, focus on what you're feeling. Don't spend time worrying about what your partner thinks. That being said, you should definitely ask your partner how they feel about the therapist after you've accessed yourself. The goal is to find a therapist that makes both of you feel respected and comfortable.

Conclusion

I hope this book was able to help you to learn how to become the perfect lover that you have always wanted to become and that your partner has always dreamt of having.

The next step is to start practicing what you have learnt in this book in your everyday life.

Remember that keeping your love and relationship not only alive but also interesting should be your main priority in any lasting relationship. It means that you have to dedicate some time to being a good lover and a passionate, compassionate, and attentive lover. It means you continuously learn what makes your lover tick mentally, emotionally and sexually. If you can get this right, I can guarantee that you will be the best lover there is and your love and relationship can and will stand the test of time.